Beauty and Horror in a Concentration Camp

Published by New City Press
202 Comforter Blvd.,
Hyde Park, NY 12538
www.newcitypress.com

©2022 New City Press

Beauty and Horror in a Concentration Camp
The Story of Etty Hillesum

Cover design and layout by Miguel Tejerina

Library of Congress Control Number: 2022900589

ISBN: 978-1-56548-524-2 (paper)
ISBN: 978-1-56548-525-9 (e-book)

Printed in the United States of America

Beauty and Horror in a Concentration Camp

The Story of Etty Hillesum

James Murphy

New City Press
Hyde Park, New York

Contents

Introduction

A combination of sex, religion, and violence is usually the makings of a good story, and Etty Hillesum's life certainly had all of that. She was a promiscuous Jewish woman who succeeded in dramatically turning her life around, and was murdered before the age of thirty. But that is not the reason I want to tell her story—at least not the main one! What attracts me to her is her mysticism and her astonishing interior joy in the face of the unspeakable atrocities of the Second World War. More people should know her amazing story, a journey that began in Holland and ended in the Auschwitz-Birkenau concentration and extermination camp in German-occupied Poland, where she was killed in November 1943. Most Americans have scarcely even heard of her.

I was one of those Americans myself. Up to a few years ago I barely knew who she was, until a cousin gave me a spiritual book as a gift for my fiftieth anniversary of ordination. Titled *God's Passionate Desire* by William A. Barry, S.J., the book is a collection of retreat reflections, one of which briefly tells Etty Hillesum's story.[1] The passages Fr. Barry quotes from her diary moved me deeply, passages about how she handled the humiliation and isolation that Jews suffered in the Netherlands at that time. When she learned one afternoon that she could not even take a walk in the park anymore, her reaction was not what most of us would feel. "And everywhere signs barring Jews from the paths and the open country," she wrote. "But above the one narrow path still left to us stretches the sky intact. . . . I find life beautiful, and I feel free. The sky within me is as wide as the one stretching above my head."[2]

Sections like that one caused me to buy a copy of her diary, and I continued to be astonished at her writing. "The misery here is quite terrible," she wrote from Westerbork transit camp shortly before she was killed. "And yet late at night, when the day has slunk away into the depths behind me, I often walk with a spring in my step along the barbed wire. And then, time and again, it soars straight from my heart—I can't help it, that's just the way it is, like some elemental force—the feeling that life is glorious and magnificent, and that one day we shall be building a whole new world."[3]

Unusual words those, coming from a concentration camp. They are, as Fr. Barry points out, the words of a mystic! As I read them, I couldn't help thinking of other Jews who suffered the same fate as Etty, but with very different feelings. I thought in particular of Elie Wiesel attending a Jewish New Year (Rosh Hashanah) celebration in Auschwitz that his fellow prisoners organized. It included a call to bless God's name, a standard prayer for such celebrations. Wiesel would have been familiar with it, as an Orthodox Jew, but in this particular setting he wasn't ready for it. Not in a concentration camp! "Why, but why would I bless Him," he wrote later. "Every fiber in me rebelled. Because He caused thousands of children to burn in His mass graves? Because He kept six crematoria working day and night, including Sabbath and Holy Days? . . . I was the accuser, God the accused. My eyes had opened and I was alone, terribly alone in a world without God, without man. Without love or mercy."[4]

Wiesel survived World War II and went on to live a long and productive life (he authored over fifty books), but the question of faith in God continued to haunt him. The Jewish survivors of the death camps, he said in an address in 1972, "had every reason in the world to deny God . . . every reason in the world to become ferocious nihilists, anarchists, carriers of fear and nightmare."[5] Wiesel did not reject God outright, however, but there are other Jewish intellectuals of the Holocaust who did. Richard Rubenstein, an American Jewish theologian, for example, said this in response to the horrors perpetrated by the Nazis:

> God really died at Auschwitz. . . . [N]othing in human choice, decision, value or meaning can any longer have vertical reference to transcendent standards. We are alone in a silent, unfeeling cosmos. . . . Though most of us will refrain from antisocial behavior, we do so because of fear of ourselves and others rather than fear of God. . . . Ultimately, as with all things, it will pass away, for omnipotent Nothingness is Lord of All Creation.[6]

I do not mean to pass judgment on people like Wiesel and Rubenstein. Most of us would feel the way they did. But Etty Hillesum was a clear example of someone who did not. Not that she didn't share Wiesel's horror at what was happening around her—she called the Nazi policies "demonic."[7] But at the same time she insisted that "there must be someone to live through it all and bear witness to the fact that God lived, even in these times. And why should I not be that witness?"[8]

Typed Sheets and a Rusty Paperclip

The reason Etty's story is not better known has to do with the decisions of publishers. The writings of people like Elie Wiesel and Anne Frank and Viktor Frankl found their way into print soon after the war because publishers found them to be concise and readable. They considered Etty Hillesum's stream-of-consciousness style too repetitive and too philosophical. The result was that her ten tattered notebooks, written in longhand, gathered dust in the attic of a friend, Klaas Smelik, for almost forty years before they saw the light of day. Eventually, Smelik's son Klaas A. D. Smelik picked up the cause and sent a sample of the diary to a publisher by the name of Jan Geurt Gaarlandt who said he would take a look at it.

That sample, which Gaarlandt described as a "small pile of letters and sheets of typed text held together by a rusty paperclip," sat on his desk for three more years before he finally got around to doing something with it.[9] When he finally began to read it, he was immediately captivated. "The very first sentences I read fascinated and shocked me, and they have remained with me ever since," he wrote later.[10]

The result was an abridged version of the diary called *Etty Hillesum: An Interrupted Life*, which appeared in Dutch in 1981 and in English in 1984. Then, in 1986, the full text of her diary and letters were published in Dutch, followed by an English version in 2002, with the title *Etty: The Letters and Diaries of Etty Hillesum 1941–1943, Complete and Unabridged*. Her writings are now available in over sixty languages. The abridged version, *An Interrupted Life*, continues to be more popular because of its brevity. The 800-page unabridged version (including 900 annotations) tends to be the focus of scholars who appreciate the full depth and complexity of her writing. For well over a decade now, these scholars have been doing intense study of her writings, and three International Etty Hillesum Conferences have been organized in Europe, two at Ghent University in Belgium (2008 and 2014), and one in Middelburg, the Netherlands (2018), bringing together experts from Canada, the United States, Ireland, Great Britain, Portugal, Spain, France, and the Low Countries. The proceedings of those conferences have been published in three volumes, and those books are an indispensable resource for anyone wishing to write about Etty Hillesum. But they are expensive and highly academic; the three volumes together cost about $900. Like the unabridged edition of her diary, they are not the kinds of books ordinary readers buy or read.

It should not be a surprise, then, that Etty Hillesum is still not well known outside the walls of academia—at least not in the United States. That may be why Pope Benedict XVI wanted to call attention to her in one of his last public talks before retiring in 2013.[11] Quoting from her diary, the pope held up the example of this young Jewish woman whose journey began so far from God and ended so near him. She found God deep down within herself, the pope said. *L'Osservatore Romano* has also featured her spiritual journey a number of times. One article published in 2012 focused on the encounter Etty Hillesum had with another mystic and Auschwitz victim, St. Edith Stein.[12] That article wonders what nonverbal communication might have passed between the two as their eyes met in Westerbork in 1942. It is speculation, of course. We know that the two noticed each other during Edith's four-day stay in the camp en route to Auschwitz. Etty mentions it in her diary, referring to Edith as the nun "from that rich, strictly orthodox and highly talented family in Breslau."[13] But as for how much communication there was between the two, we can only surmise. Meeting or not, Etty Hillesum and Edith Stein are among the most interesting intellectuals of the twentieth century. We will devote a full chapter to comparing the two.

Our journey will also include people who survived the Holocaust, such as writers like Viktor Frankl and Elie Wiesel. These witnesses are important because they fill in the gaps in our knowledge of Auschwitz-Birkenau extermination camp and give us a good idea of what daily life was like when Etty Hillesum and Edith Stein were taken there. Etty herself has left us ample descriptions of Westerbork, but if she wrote anything about Auschwitz it has not survived.

The Auschwitz killing center was indeed a gruesome place, and I will not shy away from describing it: the starvation, the slave labor, the gas chambers, the unhygienic conditions, the mass graves into which Edith Stein and (presumably) Etty Hillesum were dumped. To water down that history, or to evade it, would dishonor the memory of those victims. It is a story that too many people today know little about. Some even deny that it ever happened. According to a 2020 survey of millennials and Gen Z adults, nearly two thirds of US young adults were unaware that six million Jews died in the Holocaust. Almost a quarter (23 percent) said they believed the Holocaust was either a myth, or had been exaggerated, or they weren't sure; and almost half (49 percent) said they had seen Holocaust denial or distortion posts online.[14] A similar display of ignorance is becoming apparent in Europe—even at a site as sacred as the Auschwitz-Birkenau memorial and museum. In October 2021, vandals sprayed slurs denying the Holocaust on nine of the barracks there.[15]

General Dwight Eisenhower foresaw the possibility that future generations would try to dismiss descriptions of the camps and Nazi atrocities as propaganda. At the end of the war, he made a point of going to see one of the concentration camps (Ohrdruf, about thirty miles west of Buchenwald) for himself. He ordered American soldiers and German civilians to go to the camps, in addition to inviting American journalists and members of Congress to do the same.

A Catholic (Christian) Perspective

The reader should be aware of the lens through which I will interpret the life of Etty Hillesum. This story will be told from a Catholic viewpoint, despite the criticism of some experts that we Catholics are too eager to "canonize" Etty, or turn her into one of our own. Etty Hillesum, those critics say, cannot be categorized or taken over by any particular religious tradition, Catholic or otherwise.[16] That is indeed true. Different writers see different sides to her life. As the introduction to the Proceedings of the 2008 Etty Hillesum Conference points out, it is remarkable how many scholars compare her with personages of widely different backgrounds, from German pastor Dietrich Bonhoeffer and Danish theologian Soren Kierkegaard to German writer Franz Kafka and American philosopher William J. Durant.

By approaching Etty Hillesum's life from a Catholic perspective, I do not intend to "claim" her, but to explore how it was that Etty, an assimilated Jew steeped in the culture of the Christian Enlightenment in Europe, drew inspiration from the Christian tradition.[17] Doing so from a Catholic perspective—the only one I have—allows me to use the vocabulary shared by these Christian authors to describe the transformation Etty experienced in her inner life. The most influential authors in her life were, indeed, not Jewish but Christian: people like Rainer Maria Rilke, Carl Jung, St. Augustine of Hippo, Fyodor Dostoevsky, and Meister Eckhart. With those writers in the background and the help of a skillful therapist in the foreground, Etty Hillesum went through a remarkable transformation that moved from her head to her heart, from excessive intellectualizing to total surrender before "a power greater than any ever I knew."[18] That surrender was a turning point in her search for God, and it was the gateway to her mysticism.

As a Catholic, I would make two further observations. It is readers who have experienced that surrender in their own lives who are most likely to notice its implications in her life. And those readers are most likely to see her transformation as the work of God rather than the work of Etty herself. From the Catholic (and Christian) perspective, Etty Hillesum's story is a story about the work of the Holy Spirit. And that is the case whether Etty herself was aware of it or not. The initiative was God's, not hers, as it is with anyone who undertakes such important internal labor. It is a question of faith, not academic research (although rigorous research is also very important). In the words of Sister Jean Dwyer, O.P., in her book *The Unfolding Journey: The God Within: Etty Hillesum & Meister Eckhart*: "Her writings show us a very human and flawed individual chosen by God to soar to the heights of mystical union."[19] And in this case, let it be noted, God chose someone outside the Christian tradition. You don't have to be a Christian to be a mystic.

Authentic mysticism has two elements: a loving knowledge of God which comes from a personal encounter with the divine, and a way of life that leads to a loving union with the Mystery that is at the core of life.[20] That is a rough description, of course, not a precise definition, because a precise definition is difficult to come by. As the encyclopedia *Sacramentum Mundi* states, the Catholic Church "has never made any universal and binding declarations on the exact nature of true mystical experience. Revelation and the Church remain a *norma negativa* for mystical assertions."[21] In other words, the Church is more inclined to say what mysticism is *not* than what it is. At the same time, however, experts on the spiritual life say that mysticism is not some esoteric state that is confined to the privileged few. Mystical experiences may be more common than most people realize, and they are not confined to Christians. The Church is careful to give "respectful consideration to non-Christian mysticism."[22]

Etty Hillesum is in that non-Christian category. Exploring how she got there is the work of this book.

A Note on the Word "Holocaust"

Many Jewish writers and historians, with reason, object to the use of the word *Holocaust* when referring to the annihilation of six million Jews during the Second World War. The reason is the theological and historical background of *holocaust*, which refers to a religious sacrifice. The intention of the Nazis was not to offer a sacrifice to some God. For this reason, the word *Holocaust* is used less and less in Europe today. The Hebrew word *Shoah*, meaning "catastrophe," is used instead. When Pope Benedict XVI spoke about Etty Hillesum in 2013, he used Shoah in order to show respect for those who suffered in the concentration camps of World War II.

But Holocaust does continue to be used. The *Encyclopedia of the Holocaust*, published by the Yad Vashem Memorial in Jerusalem, for example, does not use Shoah in place of Holocaust. Neither does *The Holocaust Encyclopedia*, published by Yale University Press. The editors of those encyclopedias made that decision for a good reason. Most people in the English-speaking world have not heard the word *Shoah*, let alone know what it means. As Walter Laqueur, editor of the Yale encyclopedia, points out in its preface, "In the English-speaking world the word [Holocaust] is so deeply rooted that it is impractical to deviate from it."[23]

In this book, we follow the lead of those encyclopedias. Clarity of language demands that we use the word everyone knows. But we do so while being fully aware of its limitations and with the utmost respect for those who suffered the horrors of Nazi Germany.

A Brief Chronology

15 January 1914: Etty Hillesum was born in the Netherlands.

March 1937: As a college student, Etty moved into the house of Han Wegerif with whom she would have an affair.

9 November 1938: The Night of Broken Glass, when thousands of Jewish businesses and synagogues in Germany and Austria were destroyed, and hundreds of Jews were arrested and sent to concentration camps.

15 May 1940: Holland capitulated to the Nazis.

3 February 1941: Etty met Julius Spier, who immediately became her therapist and lover.

9 March 1941: Etty made her first entry in her diary, describing in graphic detail her interior chaos and need for counseling.

March 1942: Two gas chambers, known as the "Little Red House" and the "Little White House," opened in Birkenau. Much bigger gas chambers would be opened the following year.

3 July 1942: The tone of her diary changed; Etty began to look death in the eye.

30 July 1942: Etty began work at Westerbork concentration camp.

First week of August 1942: Etty met St. Edith Stein during Stein's brief stay at Westerbork en route to Auschwitz.

15 September 1942: Julies Spier died in Amsterdam. Etty was in the city at the time due to sickness; she spent most of the winter of 1942–43 in Amsterdam.

13 October 1942: Etty's diary as we know it ended.

6 June 1943: Etty left Amsterdam for the last time. By this time, she had left her diary with a friend for safekeeping.

21 June 1943: Etty's parents and brother arrived in Westerbork.

7 September 1943: Etty, her parents, and her brother were put on a cattle train for Auschwitz.

30 November 1943: Etty died in Auschwitz.

Chapter 1

Who was Etty Hillesum?
Emancipated, Educated, Urbane

Etty Hillesum was born into a middle-class Jewish family in Middelburg, in the southwestern Netherlands, on 15 January 1914. Religion didn't play an important role in her upbringing. The Hillesums were assimilated Jews who lived in a house full of books where the discourse at the dinner table was both learned and secular. Etty's father, Louis Hillesum, held a master's degree in classical languages, *cum laude*, from the University of Amsterdam, his native city, and after graduation succeeded in having his thesis (about the ancient Greek historian Thucydides) accepted for publication. He went on to teach Greek and Latin in three different Dutch towns, where initially he had difficulty controlling large classes because of his poor hearing and poor vision. Eventually he got a classics post in an exclusive high school in the eastern town of Deventer where he was appointed deputy headmaster and then headmaster in 1928.

Etty's mother, Riva Bernstein, was a refugee who fled her native Russia after an anti-Jewish pogrom, and she had a respectable level of education also. In the Netherlands she was listed as a Russian teacher. (The other members of her family followed her to Amsterdam, but later immigrated illegally to the United States.) Louis and Riva married in 1912 and had three children. Esther (Etty) was born in 1914, Jacob (Jaap) in 1916, and Michael (Mischa) in 1920. All three children were exceptionally intelligent, although Etty's grades were never as high as those of her brothers. According to Jan Geurt Gaarlandt, who published the abbreviated version of Etty's diary, Jaap discovered several new vitamins at the age of seventeen for which he won admission to the national academic laboratories, an unusual honor for a student. He went on to study medicine at the University of Amsterdam and later at Leiden. His younger brother, Mischa, was a talented musician who played Beethoven in public at the age of six, and was considered by many to be one of the most promising pianists in Europe.[24] At the age of eleven, Mischa moved to Amsterdam to study at the famous Vossius Gymnasium where he became an accomplished pianist and composer; his compositions have been preserved. The famous Dutch pianist George van Renesse (1909–1994) was his mentor.[25]

Etty and her brothers spent their childhood moving with the family from town to town as her father changed jobs. She was starting fifth grade when he got his permanent job in Deventer in 1924, and after primary grades she attended the high school where he was deputy headmaster. Her studies included Hebrew, and for a while she attended meetings of the Zionist young people's group in Deventer. She was "witty, vivid, eager to read books and to study philosophy, and in these ways she was far ahead of her school friends," says Gaarlandt.[26] In 1932, she graduated from her father's school and went to the University of Amsterdam, first completing a master's degree in Dutch law in 1939, and then studying Slavic languages, an interest she inherited from her Russian mother. Because of the war, she was unable to complete a degree in that field, but continued to study Russian till the end of her life. To support herself, she gave classes in Russian, apparently with considerable success—one of the Russian language professors recommended her classes and sent students to her.[27] At the social level, she was much admired and had a wide circle of loyal friends. She was, as one commentator put it, "a young woman of her time: emancipated, educated, urbane, with professional ambitions and a penchant for bohemian lifestyles."[28]

Two Lovers at Once

In Amsterdam Etty found lodging in a variety of places, sometimes sharing rooms with her brothers who had also come there to study. Finally, in March 1937, she moved into a room in the spacious house of a sixty-two-year-old accountant, Han Wegerif, who hired her "as a sort of housekeeper."[29] Her room was in the front of the house on the third floor, overlooking the famous Museum Square in South Amsterdam. It was in this room-with-a-view that Etty wrote most of her diary. Although she was hired as a housekeeper, she soon began a romantic relationship with Wegerif (who was a widower), despite the difference in age and the presence of his twenty-one-year-old son who was also a boarder in the house. Some of the boarders became close friends of Etty's, especially Maria Tuinzing, to whom Etty gave her diary before she left Amsterdam for the last time, with instructions that she pass it on to Klaas Smelik.

Etty also entered a second sexual relationship at this time. When invited by one of the boarders to attend a session with a psycho-chirologist (palmist) by the name of Julius Spier, she went along, probably out of curiosity. The session, on 3 February 1941, turned out to be a life-altering experience for Etty. She immediately asked to begin therapy sessions with Spier, then became his assistant and lover while continuing her relationship with Wegerif. She was twenty-seven years old and he was fifty-four. It was Spier (to whom she refers as "S" in her writing) who suggested that she begin keeping a diary as a therapeutic exercise, which she did over the next eighteen months. What she ended up producing, however, was more than a run-of-the-mill account of her daily activities. It was a tour de force. As biographer Patrick Woodhouse writes:

> Through recording the complex ups and downs of her story, by tracing the contours of her own intensely alive inner life, by reflecting on what she was reading, by describing and confronting her own moods, the diary created a psychological space in which she could take stock of who she was and what was happening around her and within her. In this discipline of diary-keeping in which her natural talent as a writer flowered, she brought to bear her fierce intelligence and her single-minded determination to address within herself what she knew needed to be attended to if she was ever going to find any mental peace and rest.[30]

Who Was Julius Spier?

But it wasn't just the diary that helped her find the mental peace she sought. Etty's remarkable transformation happened under the direction of her new friend, the irrepressible Julius Spier. Born in Frankfurt, Germany, the sixth of seven children in a Jewish family, Spier was a peculiar genius. At the age of fourteen, he became an apprentice in a beer trading firm and worked his way up to the position of manager. He also set up his own publishing house on the side and pursued studies in a field that commanded respect at the time: chirology, the practice of psychoanalyzing people through the reading of their palms (today it is considered pseudoscience at best).

Eventually Spier resigned his position with the beer firm and moved to Zurich, where he spent two years studying psychoanalysis and chirology under Carl Jung. Jung wrote the introduction to Spier's book, written at this time, which was entitled *The Hands of Children*. Spier gave numerous lectures on chirology in Switzerland, Germany, and the Netherlands, illustrating his talks with thousands of slides of handprints, including the handprints of prominent people such as Jung, Albert Einstein, and Auguste Rodin.[31]

On Jung's recommendation, Spier eventually set up a formal practice in psycho-chirology in Berlin with significant success; he also taught classes. His practice closed, however, following the cataclysmic attack on Jews on the night of 9 November 1938—what became known as the "Night of Broken Glass" (*Kristallnacht*) because of the glass that was broken in thousands of Jewish storefronts, homes, and synagogues. Tens of thousands of Jews were terrorized in their homes by mobs or arrested and sent to concentration camps. For Julius Spier, it was time to get out. He left Germany legally by paying off some highly placed Nazis whom he had treated as patients, which meant he could take most of his considerable fortune with him.[32]

Spier set up shop in Amsterdam where he soon became a pied piper with a new band of followers: many Dutch students, especially women, gathered around him, dazzled by his dynamic personality and engaging lectures. He continued to practice his psycho-chirology and psychoanalysis, and his therapy included a surprising component. He engaged in a type of eroticized wrestling with his patients on the floor. At the time, some therapists believed that psychoanalysis was more effective when there was a physical bond between the therapist and the patient.[33] Etty's diary describes one such tussle in which she succeeded in overcoming him despite his large size, giving him a bleeding lip.[34] "No one had ever been able to do that to him before and he could not conceive how I had managed it," she wrote. "It all seemed so innocent, this wrestling, new and unexpected, and so liberating. It was not until later that it took hold of my fantasies."[35] Liberating or not, it was indeed unusual.

By this time Spier's marriage had long since broken up. He divorced his wife of seventeen years in 1934, leaving their two children with her. Following this departure, he had a number of affairs before becoming engaged to one of his students, Hertha Levi, who immigrated to London shortly before he immigrated to Amsterdam; the two stayed in contact and fully intended to marry. When Spier and Etty met, there was no effort by either of them to conceal the truth about a second sexual partner. In fact, if Spier the therapist was promiscuous, Etty the patient was well able to keep up with him. "I am accomplished in bed," she wrote in the first entry to her diary, "just about seasoned enough I should think to be counted among the better lovers, and love does indeed suit me to perfection." She added however that sex for her was a "mere trifle, set apart from what is truly essential" in life.[36] Clearly there was more to this young woman than her physical desires.

"Many details of Etty Hillesum's personality are fascinating," Maria Clara Lucchetti Bingemer said at the 2014 Etty Hillesum Conference. "A young, beautiful and refined woman, she was very attractive to men, and had, even at a young age, many admirers and boyfriends. She was cultivated, extremely brilliant intellectually, multi-lingual, well-read in German and Russian literature, and an accomplished writer."[37]

Of all her boyfriends, Spier turned out to be the most important, not as a lover but as a therapist and spiritual mentor. His influence in the life of Etty Hillesum cannot be overstated. It was he who introduced her to the Gospel of Matthew, the Letters of St. Paul, and St. Augustine, while at the same time bringing order to her emotional chaos. As we will see in this chapter and the next, Spier must be given credit for his part in

Etty's astonishing journey from confusion and a lack of direction to self-assurance and conviction.

Her Father's Secret Affair

Many people confided in Etty, sometimes sharing their most intimate secrets with her, despite her young age. A remarkable example was Christine van Nooten, one of Etty's old teachers. Christine and Etty's father had a secret affair while they were working at the same school in Deventer, and Etty was the only one who knew about it.[38] Such was the trust Christine placed in her.

The world would never have known about this affair were it not for a meeting that took place between publisher Jan Geurt Gaarlandt and Christine van Nooten shortly after the publication of the Dutch version of *An Interrupted Life* in 1981.[39] During that visit (at Christine's home) she put a box on the table which appeared to be empty until she took out the false bottom to reveal a collection of letters hidden underneath. Those letters, she said, were an exchange of correspondence between Louis Hillesum (Etty's father) and herself, expressions of a great love that had blossomed between them toward the end of their time in Deventer. With some amusement, she invited Gaarlandt to read some of the letters, knowing full well he couldn't do so without help. They were written in Greek!

That day, Christine asked Gaarlandt to publish the letters after her death, a request to which Gaarlandt happily agreed. As it turned out, the letters were never printed. Christine later burned them at the suggestion of a priest who went to see her regularly during her last years.[40] We do not know how much Etty knew about the letters but, in any case, her knowledge of this affair did not lessen her respect and love for her parents.[41] At the same time, she kept in contact with Christine. Her last piece of writing that we know of was a postcard she threw out the window of the train bound for Auschwitz on 7 September 1943. It was addressed to Christine van Nooten.

Attraction to the Contemplative Life

Monastic life fascinated Etty Hillesum. When struggling with sexual feelings one Sunday night, she wondered what people in monasteries do when they are tempted. "And I suddenly understood those monks who flagellate themselves to tame their sinful flesh," she wrote.[42] In other diary entries she referred to her "small monkish bed," and when kneeling to pray one night she described the walls of her room as "austere and plain like a monastery cell's."[43] Later, when a group of priests and nuns—dressed in their religious habits with a Star of David on the left breast— arrived unexpectedly at Westerbork transit camp when Etty worked there, she had many questions about monastic life and what led to their arrest. In her diary she called it "a remarkable day."[44]

"Sometimes I long for a convent cell," she wrote in August 1941, "with the sublime wisdom of centuries set out on bookshelves all along the wall and a view across the cornfields—there must be cornfields and they must wave in the breeze—and there I would immerse myself in the wisdom of the ages and in myself."[45] In a later entry she wrote about her desire to lock herself in a room for several days and not talk to anybody. "One ought to pray, day and night, for the thousands," she wrote. "One ought not to be without prayer for even a single moment."[46] Thoughts like these have led some Catholics to wonder if Etty might have become a Carmelite nun (like St. Edith Stein), had she lived long enough. That might be wishful thinking, however. Etty was indeed attracted to "the seclusion of a nunnery," but she also said, "I know that I must seek You among the people, out in the world."[47]

Her Favorite Writers

As it turned out, Etty immersed herself in the wisdom of the ages without ever entering a convent. She was a voracious reader, a bookworm who read the classics like her life depended on them. By one count she quotes about twenty different philosophers and literary figures in her diary and letters. Here are some of her favorites:

Rainer Maria Rilke (1875–1926): This German poet is considered by many one of the most gifted poets in the modern era. Etty found refuge in his poetry when she was having a bad day, and she quotes him frequently in her diary—120 times by one count. He was like a soulmate to her, and the parallels between the two writers explain that affinity.[48] Both experienced a difficult upbringing. Both loved the wide-open plains of Russia and Russian culture, although Etty never went there. Both read Meister Eckhart and Russian novelists like Leo Tolstoy and Fyodor Dostoevsky. Both admired Francis of Assisi. (Rilke presents St. Francis as a kind of deity at the end of *The Book of Hours*.[49]) Both treasured solitude. Both were intense thinkers who searched for God in the inner world of the mind and heart. And both addressed God directly, one in her diary and the other in his poems. The writer of the diary found the language of the poet energizing, even life-giving. Rilke's groping in the dark resonated with Etty as she groped for answers during World War II.

Fyodor Dostoevsky (1821–1881): Etty began reading this Russian novelist at the age of twelve, and she became deeply interested in the religious themes for which he is famous.[50] His name or his novels are mentioned thirty-five times in her diary and letters, which makes him the second most-quoted author after Rilke.[51] One of her favorite novels was *The Idiot*, a story about an open-hearted prince whose guilelessness causes the people around him to call him stupid—an idiot! Something about that novel enchanted her. "I have a new friend: Prince Myshkin," she wrote. "I don't know much about him yet, but he already has a firm place in my thoughts."[52] When she thought about ending up in a concentration camp, she decided that the two volumes of *The Idiot* would have to be among the books she would pack between the clothes. "I would gladly make do with a little less food if only I could get the books in," she wrote.[53]

But Etty also loved Dostoevsky's last novel, *The Brothers Karamazov*. In fact, *The Brothers Karamazov* had a more significant influence on her than *The Idiot*, as we will see later, although she does not mention the former novel by name as often.

Carl Jung (1875–1961): The Swiss psychiatrist and psychoanalyst became famous for his research into the hidden, pre-rational side of the psyche—what we call the subconscious. Etty learned about him from Julius Spier, and the fact that she quoted him frequently should not be surprising. After all, Jung was the expert on the world within, and it was there that Etty looked in her search for clarity. Her spiritual journey began as a psychological one as she confronted her inner demons.[54] "People know the immensities of outer space better than they know their own depths," she wrote in June 1941, echoing Jung's words.[55] And four months later she wrote: "The feeling that there is a dream world and a grey, everyday world, and that the two are irreconcilable. And I do so want to reconcile them, I want to live them both at the same time. I know it can be done."[56] That too is Jungian language, like the "two worlds" or realities of our lives which Jung described—an example of the influence he had on Etty.

St. Augustine of Hippo (354–430): This bishop is arguably the most influential figure in the history of Western Christianity. His focus on the human being's innate need for God appealed to Etty, in particular his teaching that there is a faculty in humans that transcends time and space, an immortal soul that bears a likeness to God. "You made us for yourself and our hearts find no peace until they rest in you," he famously wrote in the *Confessions*.[57] Etty was aware of that prayer; in one diary entry (30 May 1942), she quotes two paragraphs from the *Confessions* in which Augustine warns against the danger of clinging to worldly creatures, because in them "there is no resting, for they do not last."[58]

In a later chapter Augustine says more about the sinful habit of clinging to things, and how they enslaved him. The impulses of nature were at war with the impulses of the spirit, he wrote, and the impulses of nature kept winning even though he was revolted by them. "For my will was perverse and lust had grown from it, and when I gave in to lust, habit was born, and when I did not resist the habit it became a necessity. These were the links which together formed what I have called my chain, and it held me fast in the duress of servitude."[59] As we will see in the next chapter, Etty saw a similar servitude in her early relationship with Julius Spier.

Meister Eckhart (c. 1260–1328): The medieval mystic had a profound knowledge of the human heart (like St. Augustine) and a burning desire to find out what it is in human beings that makes them desire God. We humans are fragile creatures, he taught, begotten "in bed" and subject to all sorts of primitive instincts and weaknesses, and yet we have within us a divine spark, a hint of immortality. Our souls were created in the image and likeness of God, he said, echoing St. Augustine and the fathers of the early Church. Our souls are the place where time and eternity meet, where we touch the mystery of the next life while still in this life. This insight can be detected in Etty's diary also. She liked to refer to people as creatures made in God's image and, like Eckhart, she saw a hint of immortality in that image. She does not use theological language to describe it, but it is implied in her frequent use of the word "eternity." Here are some examples:

"This sort of feeling has been growing much stronger in me: a hint of eternity steals through my smallest daily activities and perceptions."[60]

"It is in these moments—and I am so grateful for them— that all personal ambition drops away from me, that my thirst for knowledge and understanding comes to rest, and that a small piece of eternity descends on me with a sweeping wingbeat."[61]

"At night the barracks sometimes lay in the moonlight, made out of silver and eternity: like a plaything that had slipped from God's preoccupied hand."[62]

The Bible

The influence of Scripture reached Etty Hillesum through her favorite writers, but it also came directly from the Bible itself. Etty loved reading the Bible, a habit she learned from Spier. She mentions the Bible thirty-three times in her diary and letters, which puts it third in importance after Rilke and Dostoevsky.[63] "Something elemental flows out of the Old Testament, and something homely as well," she wrote in July 1942. "Splendid people live in its pages, poetic and austere. It is really an incredibly exciting book, the Bible, rugged and tender, simple and wise."[64]

The Book of Psalms was one of her favorites. She picked up that book the way she picked up Rilke's *Book of Hours*. "Those psalms that have become part of my daily life were excellent fare on an empty stomach," she wrote in July 1942.[65] And that daily habit continued when she volunteered in Westerbork camp.[66]

She loved the New Testament also. In fact, she ranked the four Gospels near the top of her list. The Gospel of Matthew was a special favorite. "I would love to be like the lilies in the field," she wrote in one entry, quoting from the Sermon on the Mount. "Someone who managed to read this age correctly would surely have learned just this: to be like a lily in the field."[67]

Adolf Hitler Tightens the Screws

Meanwhile the anti-Semitic laws in the Netherlands were getting more ominous by the day, and Etty Hillesum must have known better than most how bad it would get. Julius Spier had seen it up close in Germany during the previous decade and must have told her about it: the laws forbidding Jews to practice professions such as law or medicine; the wholesale confiscation of Jewish businesses and property by the state; the blatant suppression of human rights. In Germany, people had been compartmentalized into two categories: Jews and Aryans. Only full-blooded Aryan Germans could be citizens of the state with rights; Jews had no rights. They could not own land, enter institutions of higher learning, hold positions of influence such as teaching or editing newspapers, or marry or have sexual relations with people of German blood. The plan was to make the lives of Jews so unbearable that they would have to leave Germany.

A similar legislative agenda was now being implemented in the Netherlands and the rest of Europe. (By June 1941, all of continental Europe, except Portugal, was under the control of Adolf Hitler or his close allies.) One of those laws, the one excluding Jews from all professions, had a particular impact on Etty and her family. She had just graduated in law. Her brother had just graduated in medicine. Her father was a schoolmaster. The law added to the long list of daily rules and regulations meant to humiliate Dutch Jews and make their lives unbearable: the rule prohibiting Jews from staying in the homes of non-Jews; the rule forbidding Jews from entering non-Jewish barber shops or shopping in non-Jewish stores outside strictly prescribed times; the rule prohibiting Jews from using public telephones, or any form of public or private transportation; the curfew that kept Jews indoors from 8 p.m. to 6 a.m.; the decree that all Jews over the age of twelve must wear a yellow star on the left breast. "Last night at seven o'clock I was cast into a hell of alarm and despondency brought on by the new regulations," Etty wrote on 1 July 1942.[68]

As this systematic harassment increased, so did reports in the press that Jews were being transported out of the Netherlands for extermination somewhere in the "east." In late June 1942, the Polish government-in-exile reported through BBC radio that 700,000 Jews had already been exterminated in German-occupied Poland.[69] The impact of this news can be seen in Etty's diary, where her writing takes on an ominous tone. She begins to face the possibility of her own death. It was at this point that she was ordered to go to Westerbork, the transit camp for Dutch Jews on their way to extermination in Poland. Over 100,000 Dutch Jews would eventually pass through it. To avoid deportation, Etty applied for a job at the Jewish Council in Amsterdam (on Jaap's suggestion), and was accepted. This council was a fake structure set up by the Nazis to give Jews the illusion that they could govern their own affairs.

Etty was immediately disgusted by the manipulation and hypocrisy she saw in the Jewish Council office. The extent to which these Jewish leaders allowed themselves to be used by the Nazi authorities shocked her. Rather than helping their fellow Jews, they were assisting the Nazi authorities in compiling census lists which were then used to send Jews to concentration camps. They were also assisting in the recruitment of able-bodied Jewish workers who were needed to fill the ever-increasing quotas in the forced labor camps, and they functioned as a center for the distribution of the humiliating Star of David badges Jews were supposed to wear. Etty was appalled. After just two weeks she quit the job and went to Westerbork as a social worker. She did this as a volunteer in the department of "Social Welfare for People in Transit" which meant she was still under the Jewish Council and, on paper at least, safe from deportation herself. In reality it meant nothing, of course. Jewish Council volunteers were eventually killed too. But Etty wanted to go to Westerbork regardless of the risks because she wanted to help her people as they faced certain death at the hands of the Nazis.

Refusal to Escape

Etty's friends were shocked and several of them tried to talk her out of going to Westerbork. Some even dreamed up elaborate plans to hide her in a safe place. One of those plans, hatched by Klaas Smelik and his daughter Joanna, involved kidnapping her from her home in Amsterdam and hiding her in their house in Hilversum, some fifteen miles from the capital. That plan never materialized because Etty refused to cooperate. On another occasion, Smelik grabbed her arm as he tried to get her to change her mind. Here are Smelik's own words:

> She wormed herself free and stood at a distance of about five feet from me. She looked at me very strangely and said, "You don't understand me."
>
> I replied: "No, I don't understand what on earth you're up to. Why don't you stay here, you fool!"
>
> Then she said: "I want to share the destiny of my people."
>
> When she said that, I knew there was no hope. She would never come to us.[70]

A Mennonite pastor, San van Drooge, who had been a student of Louis Hillesum, put together a plan to smuggle the entire Hillesum family out of Amsterdam. With the help of the underground resistance, he planned to hide them in his presbytery in Makkum, a beautiful fishing village in the northern Netherlands. But Louis Hillesum knew how stubborn his daughter could be and he did not want the rest of the family to go without her.

History has shown that these escape plans were often worth the risk. Not all those who went into hiding survived the war, of course, but many did, including Lennie Wolff, one of Etty's childhood friends. To make an escape plan work, one had to have a suitable hiding place, friends who were willing to help despite the risks to their own lives, and financial support from those friends. Etty had all of those advantages and could have reasonably expected that she would be a survivor. It is estimated that about 25,000 Jews went into hiding during World War II and about 18,000 survived the war in this way. (Anne Frank is a famous example of someone who did not survive.)[71]

The reason Etty Hillesum refused to escape, then, was not worries that the plan would not work. The reason was her sincere desire to sacrifice herself for her people, in particular to help them deal with the psychological effects of dehumanization in the concentration camps. Most victims awaiting extermination were so traumatized that they tried to escape reality by suppressing their feelings. They wanted to become like zombies just to get through one more day. Etty's mission was "to catch and stop them in their flight from themselves and then take them by the hand and lead them back to their own resources."[72] That was the core of Etty Hillesum's ethical vision, as Rachel Feldhay Brenner pointed out in the 2008 Etty Hillesum Conference. "It is a message of redemption in self-worth and self-dignity," Brenner said. "It was not the physical force of terror that she wished to defeat, but rather its insidious psychological objective of dehumanization."[73]

Preparing Herself for the Worst

This determination to resist dehumanization also applied to Etty's own life. Ten days before she went to work in Westerbork (11 July 1942), she reflected on what she would do if she herself were ordered to go to Germany. How would she act? "I wouldn't tell a soul at first," she wrote, "but retire to the quietest spot in the house, withdraw into myself and gather what strength I could from every cranny of my body and soul. I would have my hair cut short and throw my lipstick away." She would also go to see her parents and write to Spier—"the man I shall always long for." And she would pack the bare minimum into a knapsack, but make sure to include some of her beloved books. She would bring no photographs, however. Instead of photographs, she would hang the images of her loved ones on the walls of her interior castle, so that they would be close to her no matter where she ended up. Even if she found herself in a place of unimaginable cruelty, with her features "ugly and ravaged through too much suffering and too much hard work," she would always "feel safe in God's arms," she concluded.[74]

This train of thought continued the following day when she wrote one of the most memorable passages in her diary. The occasion was a horrible overnight storm that played havoc with the jasmine vines at the back of the house. As she looked down on the scene of destruction from a back window, the ruination of the jasmine became a metaphor for the ruination of her country at the hands of a brutal occupying government. But Etty refused to let that thought dehumanize her. She wrote:

Somewhere inside me the jasmine continues to blossom undisturbed, just as profusely and delicately as ever it did. And it spreads its scent round the House in which you dwell, oh God. You can see, I look after You, I bring you not only my tears and my forebodings on this stormy, gray Sunday morning, I even bring you scented jasmine. And I shall bring you all the flowers I shall meet on my way, and truly there are many of those. I shall try to make You at home always. Even if I should be locked up in a narrow cell and a cloud should drift past my small barred window, then I shall bring You that cloud, oh God, while there is still the strength in me to do so. I cannot promise You anything for tomorrow, but my intentions are good, You can see.[75]

Letters From the Camp

Etty's letters describing what went on in Westerbork transit camp are also significant pieces of writing. Along with her diary—which she continued to write in, particularly during visits home to Amsterdam—they are among the best examples of Holocaust literature anywhere, which is why scholars from around the world have gathered three times for conferences on her writings. In all, she wrote some forty letters from Westerbork, the two best-known being the long letters that were published clandestinely by the Jewish underground in the fall of 1943, shortly after Etty and her family were put on a transport to Auschwitz.

In those letters, her most vivid impression is the overcrowding: more than 10,000 people crowded "thick as flies" into a small area (119 acres) with barbed wire all around and watchtowers manned by military police armed with machine guns.[76] Basic hygiene was non-existent and dysentery was everywhere. "We have all got the 'runs,' as it is poetically termed," she writes in one letter.[77] It was a camp for people in transit to their death, she says, with "great waves of human beings constantly washed in from the cities and provinces, from rest homes, prisons, and other prison camps, from all the nooks and crannies of the Netherlands, only to be deported a few days later to meet their unknown destiny."[78] Some arrived with nothing but the slippers and underclothes they were wearing when they were rounded up, and their helplessness was heart-rending. "There was a little old woman who had left her spectacles and her medicine bottle at home on the mantel," she writes. "Could she go and get them now, and where exactly was she, and where would she be going?"[79]

"My fountain pen cannot form words strong enough to convey even the remotest picture of these transports," she writes about the trains that kept arriving jammed with people. "From the outside the impression is of bleak monotony, yet every transport is different and has its own atmosphere."[80] She was thinking of so many different stories of woe, but also so many different accents. It was like the Tower of Babel, she says: Germans with Polish accents and Germans with Russian accents, Dutch with German accents and Germans with Dutch accents.[81] She was also thinking of the mixture of social classes—upper, middle, and lower—and how the class distinction didn't disappear just because these people were in a concentration camp. Walking past tables in the barracks, she says, one could immediately tell which class a particular group belonged to just by observing their manners and the few personal belongings they had put on the table. She makes special mention of the rich and powerful, those who had everything before they were taken by the Nazis. Now, in the camp, they were no better than the poorest slum dweller who came on the same train as they did. "Their armor of position, esteem, and property has collapsed," she writes, "and now they stand in the last threads of their humanity. They exist in an empty space, bounded by earth and sky, which they must fill with whatever they can find within them—there is nothing else."[82]

A Radiant Joy

Among those traumatized victims, Etty soon became known for her joy and inner peace as she tried to assure these prisoners that God had not abandoned his people. Friedrich Weinreb, who worked in Westerbork at the same time as Etty, remembers her walking around the beds with a leather bag over her shoulder, bending down toward every sick person and asking how she could help. "What I found most striking," he wrote, "was her religious sense of things, a quality that she had recently discovered in herself. There was something about her that spoke of an ancient, primeval struggle, the weight of thousands of years—and at the same time something light and joyful."[83]

But that light-hearted joy was severely tested one day in June 1943 when her parents and her younger brother Mischa arrived on a train from Amsterdam. It broke her heart. Before long, however, Etty's practical side kicked in, and she did all she could to keep her family off the other train—the one that departed for the east every Tuesday morning. Those efforts were useless. On 7 September 1943, all four of them (Etty, her brother, and their parents) were packed into the Tuesday morning train and sent on the three-day journey to Auschwitz-Birkenau extermination camp. We will say much more about that in a later chapter.

Let us end this chapter with the words of Meins G. S. Coetsier, an expert who spoke at the 2008 Etty Hillesum Conference about the impact Etty's writing has had on him personally:

Etty Hillesum's lasting legacy of mystical thoughts in her writings not only moved me; they changed my life . . . forcing me to discover the depth of my own humanity. Reading Hillesum became more and more mesmerizing to me. I recalled her experiences and wondered why the writing of this Dutch woman, who grew up not far from where I lived, had achieved such extraordinary, culture-defining impact. What possible ingredient in that horrific place and time gave rise to the transcendent, to visionary diaries and letters that could endlessly stir people's hearts over decades?[84]

I am one of those whose heart was stirred by Etty Hillesum's writings, although I was born and grew up a little further away, in Ireland. Our lives overlapped, but just barely. I was ten months old when Etty was dying in Auschwitz in 1943. Getting to know her—and write about her—has been one of the great blessings of my life.

Chapter 2

The Struggle to Find Herself: Confronting Her Inner Chaos

Reading Etty Hillesum's diary is a bit like reading *The Confessions of St. Augustine*. In that famous autobiography, Augustine draws a dark picture of his sinful youth, so dark that, as one commentator says, the reader could easily lose sight of the good qualities which he certainly possessed as a young man.[85] All his life Augustine was an affectionate son who never uttered a harsh word against his mother, despite breaking away from her control as a young man. He also showed exceptional loyalty to the mistress with whom he lived for many years, and he was truly fond of Adeodatus, the son she bore him. In the *Confessions*, he does not give himself enough credit for these feelings.

There is a similar lack of balance in the early part of Etty Hillesum's diary. Her startling honesty and use of vivid language could cause the reader to visualize her as unstable and lose sight of the successful side of her life. After all, Etty did complete a degree in law at the University of Amsterdam and she gave successful classes in Russian to support herself. She also had a wide circle of very loyal friends, many of whom were deeply worried when she refused opportunities to escape the Nazi state. Etty does in fact briefly mention that positive side of her life, but immediately adds a caveat. "I am blessed enough intellectually to be able to fathom most subjects, to express myself clearly on most things," she writes. "I seem to be a match for most of life's problems, *and yet* deep down something like a tightly wound ball of twine binds me relentlessly, and at times I am nothing more or less than a miserable, frightened creature, despite the clarity with which I can express myself"[86] (italics are mine).

The truth is that Etty Hillesum was not crazy, or some kind of sex maniac. But she did have some emotional problems, and she describes them graphically in her diary. Even allowing for exaggeration, she seems to have had unusually dark periods, days when she was in psychological pain. Here is one example (from September 1941): "On days like this, I am sure that no one suffers as much as I do. Imagine somebody in pain all over his body, unable to bear anyone touching him even with the tip of a finger—that's the feeling in my soul or whatever you want to call it."[87]

Where was this pain coming from? Was it depression and anxiety caused by living under the Nazi regime? Did her intense personality, which even her doctor noticed, contribute to the heaviness of such feelings? Was something in her family background haunting her? Probably all of the above, to one extent or another. Certainly, the Nazi threat worried her, as it did all Jews. The constantly increasing list of anti-Jewish regulations left her in "a hell of alarm and despondency," she wrote in July 1942.[88] Her intense personality and anxiety probably contributed to her problems also. Sometimes her determination to get more work done left her so exhausted that she had no strength left to do the actual work. "Maybe I take myself too seriously," she wrote.[89] But her family background was probably the most significant cause of her emotional problems. Etty Hillesum had many unhappy memories of her childhood.

The Hillesum Home

Lennie Wolff had vivid memories of growing up with Etty Hillesum. They were childhood friends because both families socialized a lot when they lived in Middelburg, and the two girls frequently stayed at each other's houses. At one point, Etty went on a trip to Switzerland with the Wolffs. Lennie loved visiting the Hillesums—she had a crush on Etty's brother Jaap for a while—and when she stayed overnight, she and Etty would lie awake half the night chatting. What Lennie remembered about those days was the "delightful chaos" and "wonderful disarray" in the Hillesum home. "Etty was such a sweet girl," she remembered. "She was just like her mother, vague and a little philosophical and dreamy. It was all so intangible and went from one thing to the next until I completely lost the thread."[90] But if Lennie found this chaos delightful, Etty did not. She called her home a madhouse, and growing up there cost her "a bucket of desperate tears every night."[91] In her diary she describes a weeklong visit to see her parents in August 1941 and the bitter memories that welled up in her during it.

> I always used to go to pieces in this madhouse. Nowadays I keep everything inwardly at arm's length and try to escape unscathed. I have no impetus here to do any real work, it is as if every bit of energy were being sucked out of me. . . . It is depressing, it is tragicomic, I don't know what kind of madhouse this really is, but I know that no human being can flourish here.[92]

So exactly what kind of home was this? In most respects it was like any middle-class Jewish home that had assimilated into mainstream Dutch society. Etty's parents raised children who had a solid Jewish identity but they did not keep a kosher kitchen or attend synagogue. Etty's father Louis had no qualms about working on the Sabbath, and during the sixteen years that the family lived in Deventer he became one of the town's leading citizens. A small, quiet, and unobtrusive man "with a great deal of humor and erudition," is how one observer described him.[93] But he was also very bookish and impractical, a scholarly recluse who sometimes had difficulty dealing with the real world. Here is how Etty, with her usual blunt words, describes him in a diary entry in November 1941:

> At a fairly advanced age, my father had traded all his uncertainties, doubts, and probably also his physical inferiority complex, his insurmountable marriage problems, for philosophical ideas that, though held in perfect sincerity and full of the milk of human kindness, are totally vague. Those ideas help him to gloss over everything, to look just at the surface instead of plumbing the depths he knows full well are there, perhaps precisely because he knows it. And so he can never hope to attain clarity. Beneath the surface, his resigned philosophy simply means: O well, which of us knows anything, all is chaos within and without. And it is that very chaos that also threatens me, that I must make it my life's task to shake off instead of reverting to it time and again.[94]

Riva, Etty's Russian-born mother, in contrast, displayed a strong and extroverted personality from an early age. She was the first in her family to flee the persecution of the Jews in Russia, and in order to reach her destination in Amsterdam she disguised herself in the uniform of a soldier with her head shaved.[95] Her marriage to Louis turned out to be difficult. "Passionate, chaotic, and in almost everything quite the opposite to her husband," is how Jan Gaarlandt describes her.[96] With her curly red hair and strange Russian accent, says Patrick Woodhouse, she would have stood out on the streets of the small provincial city of Deventer.[97]

During that weeklong visit in 1941, Etty mentions a fight that suddenly erupted as she sat quietly in her bedroom trying to concentrate on her reading: "Downstairs they are screaming blue murder, with Father yelling 'Go then,' and slamming the door; that too must be absorbed, and now I am suddenly crying since I am not all that objective really and no one can breathe properly in this house; all right make the best of it then."[98]

This was ten years after she left home, and the drama and chaos she remembered from childhood still made her cry. Clearly this tempestuous home left its mark on Etty, and she laid the blame mostly on her mother. As Woodhouse observes, she "found her mother's emotional turbulence very difficult to cope with, for in it she saw a reflection of her own budding confusion. In one entry she writes with great emphasis: 'Mother is a model of what I must never become.'"[99] In another entry Etty describes her own temptation to overeat, and bemoans "that extra little morsel, that one bite too many, and yet I can't stop myself."[100] Who does she blame? Her mama! "Mother always talks about food as if nothing else mattered," she wrote. "Come on have a little more. You can't have had enough. How thin you've grown. . . . I have an unresolved antipathy for my mother, and that is precisely why I do the things I abhor in her."[101]

But if Etty's criticism of her mother was more severe than that of her father, in the end she blamed both parents for the chaos in the home. She saw them as talented—"an indescribable mixture of barbarism and culture"—but incompatible and not equipped to raise three talented children.[102] While some parents are too strict with their children, she wrote, her parents were the opposite:

> I think my parents always felt out of their depth, and as life became more and more difficult they were gradually so overwhelmed that they became quite incapable of making

up their minds about anything. They gave us children too much freedom of action, and offered us nothing to cling to. That was because they never established a foothold for themselves. And the reason why they did so little to guide our steps was that they themselves had lost their way.[103]

In a diary entry for April 1942, she describes sitting in her father's small study as a teenager and thinking to herself that the room was "untidy and impersonal as were all the rooms in all the different houses in which we ever lived."[104] For Patrick Woodhouse, that word "impersonal" is a giveaway. "It suggests," he says, "that the houses in which they lived were never places with a sense of *personal belonging* enabling members of that family to meet with one another and share life together in a human and mutually caring way. In other words, not a home."[105]

A Troubled Young Woman

The result was that Etty grew up somewhat maladjusted, given to constant bouts of depression. That becomes a theme throughout the early part of her diary, and she didn't hold back when it came to finding words to describe it:

> *9 March 1941*: "But later came a really bad fit of depression, an inescapable pressure in my skull and gloomy thoughts, much too gloomy to bear for long."[106]

> *23 March 1941*: "It started last night; then the turbulence began to swirl up inside me as vapor swirls up from a swamp. . . . I hate myself like poison, and that's all there is to it."[107]

> *30 October 1941*: "Mortal fear in every fiber. Complete collapse. Lack of self-confidence. Aversion. Panic."[108]

Not surprisingly, this chaotic household also left its mark on Etty's brothers, both of whom were as gifted as she was. Jaap, who became a medical doctor, "was intelligent, wrote poems and was attractive to women," but he was committed to psychiatric hospitals on several occasions.[109] Mischa, who had exceptional musical talent, was treated for schizophrenia and continued to be fragile, refusing to play at a concert unless his parents were present. "In the past they used to visit mental hospitals and doctors; now they attend his concerts," Etty wrote grimly.[110] Early one morning, Mischa ran away from home and put the family through some days of anguish before they finally tracked him down in the house of acquaintances in the country. But despite all the worry he caused, Etty took sides with her brother. "He left a fairly pathetic but perfectly logical letter," she wrote, "in which he wrote that he could no longer bear the atmosphere at home. . . . How right he is, that young man."[111] But witnessing the horror of seeing Mischa being carried away to an institution by force traumatized her. Her family was "riddled with hereditary disease," she wrote that day, and she vowed "that no such unhappy human being would ever spring from my womb."[112]

This then was the troubled young woman who met Julius Spier at a palmistry session on 3 February 1941. Without delay she wrote to him and poured out her soul with startling transparency:

> And when I had left you and was going back home, I wanted a car to run me over, and thought, ah, well, I must be out of my mind, like the rest of my family, something I always think when I feel the slightest bit desperate. But I know again now that I am not mad, I simply need to do a lot of work on myself before I develop into an adult and a complete human being.[113]

Her Relationship with Julius Spier

Etty Hillesum did not hesitate. She immediately asked Spier to take her on as a patient, but it soon became obvious that there was more in play between these two than the promise of professional therapy. "But then we come to that confounded eroticism, with which he is bursting, as am I," she wrote. "As a result, we are irresistibly driven toward each other physically, though neither of us wants it, as we both once said in so many words."[114] When they "rolled around on the floor" (as part of the "wrestling" Spier engaged in with his patients), she wrote, "I would have liked to run away and weep, it felt so horrible . . . as I clung tightly to him, sensuously and yet revolted by it all."[115] And when the session was over, she wrote, all she was left with was "an embarrassed and sweating man tucking his crumpled shirt into his trousers."[116]

In this struggle with sexuality, Etty remembered the words of one of her favorite writers. The impulses of nature were at war with the impulses of the spirit, Augustine had written centuries earlier, and the impulses of nature kept winning even though he found those impulses revolting. Etty recognized the same conflict in herself. Like Augustine, her soul was torn apart by sick desires "for it wants to be and to rest with the things it loves. In them, however, there is no resting, for they do not last," she wrote.[117]

Etty knew, like Augustine, that there was something wrong with her love life, something she called her "confounded eroticism," that "small slice of chaos" that was staring at her from deep down inside her soul.[118] And when she looked back at the affairs of the past, she realized that that slice of chaos was destroying her desire for authentic love. She was disgusted with herself as she began to understand "why people get drunk or go to bed with a total stranger."[119] About a year into her therapy, she happened to meet one of her old boyfriends—a man called Max—on the street and they went for a walk together. Max noticed how Etty had changed, "had turned into a real woman," someone who was radiating wisdom, but what Etty noticed was the futility of their former relationship. "And it was the body of this man, who now walked beside me like a brother, to which I had once clung in terrible despair," she wrote.[120]

By this time, Etty had indeed changed, and so had her relationship with Spier. The tempestuous mixture of sex and therapy had given way a new self-confidence on Etty's part. She was less dependent on Spier emotionally, more able to stand on her own two feet while at the same time wishing to never abandon him. By April 1942, she was confident enough, and detached enough, to write these words: "And I shall help you and stay with you, and yet leave you entirely free. And one day I shall surrender you to the girl you mean to marry. I shall support you every step, outwardly and inwardly."[121]

Etty Hillesum and Julius Spier had become friends— "intellectual soul-mates," to use the words of Patrick Woodhouse—in a rich relationship that worked miracles in Etty's life.[122] Etty summed up the comfort level of this new friendship in an entry she made in early April 1942 that is noteworthy for its spiritual freedom and carefree joy:

> And in the evening, he now and then reads me a line of Rilke over the telephone. Just like that, at random, without any prompting. It's not a case of wanting to do something desperately, at any price, not an irresistible desire to live together. No, at this particular moment, the two of us happened to be immersed in the same things by pure chance. . . . It is all so simple, so unforced, so self-evident, so organic. We work together, I know every detail of his practice, carry the material he teaches in my head, so much so that

during a lecture I can remind him of something with just a gesture. But in addition, each of us has a private life: he has his music and I have my Russian. We don't share the same roof, we are separated by five streets, one bridge and one canal. And though we journey together, live together and become more and more united, yet we remain utterly free—I am filled with unending gratitude and surprise that my life should have turned out like this.[123]

A Remarkable Transformation

One can, with reason, dwell on the unethical side of the relationship between Etty Hillesum and Julius Spier. Spier was almost double Etty's age, and the "therapy" he practiced with her was meeting his own needs as much hers. And yet, somehow it worked. With his help, Etty learned to recognize the pain within herself, to own it and to accept it. "Be what thou art," was Spier's guiding principle, following the teaching of Carl Jung, and Etty felt personally accepted for who she was, something she never experienced growing up. "You are, in fact, the first person to whom I have ever related inwardly," she wrote.[124] That unconditional acceptance gave her a self-confidence and interior freedom that was remarkable. "He is shaping me, kneading me," she wrote. "I am being deepened and enriched. He is always there, he is the unyielding rock and my moods lap around him."[125] Two months later, when writing to a friend, she put it this way: "Well what can I tell you about myself? Did you know that on Tuesday, 3 February, I celebrated my first birthday? Because it was precisely one year ago, on 3 February 1941 that I was brought into the world by an ogre of a man wearing green plus fours and an antenna on his head."[126]

Spier was like a priest, she said. She got that idea from a novel she was reading which described a priest as a mediator between God and men. "Nothing worldly ever touched him," the novel said. "And that was why he understood the need of all who were still busy growing."[127] In a similar way, according to Etty, Spier worked hard to help people, giving each one his all despite the awareness that he could be arrested any day. "He breaks them open and draws out the poison and delves down to the sources where God hides Himself away," she wrote, adding that one could not possibly do all that work effectively if he did not live like a monk.[128]

As Etty matured, she also began to look outside herself for a mission in life, an opportunity to help others just as Spier was helping her. By this time her love for Spier had become a love for all mankind, in particular a love for her fellow Jews. This concern for her people welled up more and more within her— sometimes catching her by surprise. "This afternoon, during the Beethoven," she wrote in February of that year,

> I suddenly had to bow my head and pray for all who are lingering in freezing concentration camps, prayed God to give them strength and wished they might remember the good moments in their lives, just as in hard times I shall remember this day and many days during the last year, and draw what strength I need from them lest I become embittered with life. We must see to it that we daily grow in strength to bear the times that will come.[129]

Her move to Westerbork a few months later was the fulfill-ment of that desire to help her people.

Not long after that, on 15 September 1942, Julius Spier died of lung cancer. By chance, Etty was back in Amsterdam at the time (she had to return from Westerbork because of gallbladder problems), and her newly found emotional detachment made it easier to accept his death. Besides, she saw it as a kind of blessing because she had suspected that the Nazis would catch up with Spier sooner or later. He and his family had properties in Holland which he did not register in an effort to prevent the Nazis from confiscating them. Ironically, the SS arrived to arrest him on the day he died. According to Patrick Woodhouse, the name on his lips as he died was that of Hertha Levi, the young woman in London to whom he was engaged to be married.

Chapter 3

The Struggle to Find God: The Girl Who Learned to Kneel

In one of his last talks before he retired in 2013, Pope Benedict XVI reflected on the theme of Lent by naming three modern-day examples of interior conversion, three people who rejected the materialism of their day and found God. They were: Pavel Florenskij, the Russian scientist who grew up rejecting God but later became an Orthodox monk; Dorothy Day, the American journalist and Communist sympathizer who converted to Catholicism and founded the Catholic Worker movement; and Etty Hillesum, the hero of this book. Speaking about the third, the pope said:

> I am also thinking of Etty Hillesum, a young Dutch woman of Jewish origin who died in Auschwitz. At first far from God, she discovered him looking deep within her and she wrote: "There is a really deep well inside me. And in it dwells God. Sometimes I am there, too. But more often stones and grit block the well, and God is buried beneath. Then he must be dug out again" (*Diaries*, 97). In her disrupted, restless life she found God in the very midst of the great tragedy of the 20th century: the Shoah. This frail and dissatisfied young woman, transfigured by faith, became a woman full of love and inner peace who was able to declare: "I live in constant intimacy with God."[130]

Uncertain First Steps

But looking for God within herself wasn't always how Etty talked about this subject; that image represented an advanced stage in her faith development. Her original view of the world was that of most well-educated people of her day, a view that was secular and materialistic, with little or no reference to a deity or a loving God. At the same time, however, she was haunted by a need to search for clarity, what she called "the questioning, the discontent, the feeling that everything was empty of meaning, the sense that life was unfilled."[131] As she struggled with that angst, an experience she had one Sunday afternoon in March 1941 was an important step in the search for an answer.

That Sunday she was sitting on the dustbin under the chestnut tree at the back of the house, with the sun shining on the leafless branches and the birds chirping, when suddenly she had an epiphany, a flash of insight that changed the way she saw the world. Whereas in the past she appreciated that kind of scene with her intellect and loved to put it into words, now she simply let it happen. She became passive in the presence of mystery, and the experience filled her with emotion. "As I sat there like that in the sun," she wrote, "I bowed my head unconsciously as if to take in even more of that new feeling for life. Suddenly I knew deep down how someone can sink impetuously to his knees and find peace there, his face hidden in his folded hands."[132]

For Etty, thinking was no longer enough. She had to listen to her heart as well as her head. She had to make a break with the mindset in which she grew up, the assumption of the European Enlightenment that reason, not religion, solves the world's problems. Now, for the first time, she was questioning that assumption. "You shouldn't live on your brains alone," she wrote, "but on deeper, more abiding sources, though you should gracefully accept your brains as a precious tool for delving into what problems your soul brings forth. To put it more soberly, what all of this means for me is probably that I should have greater trust in my intuition."[133] She even went so far as to curse her brains, but then thought better of it and added: "One day I shall surely strike a balance between thinking and feeling. But this is my remedy: do not speak, do not listen to the outside world, but be perfectly still, try letting your innermost being resound, and listen to that. It is the only way."[134] The antidote to excessive intellectualization, Etty began to realize, was the ability to be comfortable with silence. To listen. To hearken.

This new way of looking at the world received strong encouragement from Julius Spier. It was he who taught her "to speak the name of God without embarrassment."[135] He also introduced her to the idea of starting and ending each day with a period of meditation, a discipline she adopted although it wasn't easy at first. "But it's not so simple, that sort of quiet hour," she wrote. "It has to be learned. A lot of unimportant inner litter and bits and pieces have to be swept out first. Even a small head can be piled high inside with irrelevant distractions. True, there may be edifying emotions and thoughts, too, but the clutter is ever present."[136]

The experience under the chestnut tree was a significant step in Etty's spiritual journey, but before long she was having second thoughts about it. On the following Sunday morning, an exact week later, she woke up in a bad mood as the familiar depression kicked in, and "the turbulence began to swirl up inside me, as vapor swirls up from a swamp." She thought about the "blessed feeling" she had experienced the previous Sunday under the chestnut tree and realized that she was not as sure about it anymore. "I no longer understand how I could have felt like that last week," she wrote, "sitting so peacefully on the dustbin in the sun."[137]

This vacillation was part of Etty Hillesum's spiritual struggle in its early stages. She would get a spiritual insight and then change her mind as she wavered back and forth between contradictory thoughts, sometimes taking one step forward and two steps back. Letting go of the rationalism in which she was raised—the intellectual basis of her life—was not easy. The result was that in the early stages of her journey, one was never sure what exactly she meant when she used the word "God." One moment God was a "handy makeshift construction," or "a primitive, primordial sound." The next, God was "that which is deepest inside me, which for the sake of convenience I call God." Eventually God would become for Etty a person, someone in whose arms she felt "so protected and sheltered and so steeped in eternity."[138]

Learning to Kneel

A month after Etty used the image of the well where God dwells inside her, she recorded another important step in her spiritual journey. This time it was not an image but a gesture, something that caught her by surprise. Let her words speak for themselves:

> This afternoon I suddenly found myself kneeling on the brown coconut matting in the bathroom, my head hidden in my dressing gown, which was slung over the broken cane chair. Kneeling doesn't really come easily to me, I feel a sort of embarrassment. Why? Probably because of the critical, rational, atheistic bit that is part of me as well. And yet every so often I have a great urge to kneel down with my face in my hands and in this way to find some peace and to listen to that hidden source within me.[139]

Etty felt embarrassed because kneeling was foreign to her tradition. It was not something Jews did during prayer, but she was now doing it despite herself. She even thought about writing a novel about this phenomenon. "What a strange story it really is, my story," she wrote, "the girl who could not kneel. Or its variation: the girl who learned to pray."[140] That novel was never written, of course, but her diary records some of the thoughts that might have gone into it:

> "Last night, shortly before going to bed, I suddenly went down on my knees in the middle of this large room . . . forced to the ground by something stronger than myself."[141]

> "A desire to kneel down sometimes pulses through my body, or rather it is as if my body had been meant and made for the act of kneeling."[142]

> "And the tears poured down my face. And that prayer gave me enough strength for the rest of the day."[143]

> "Still a lot of shame to get rid of. . . . Such things are often more intimate even than sex."[144]

Marja Clement, one of the scholars who spoke at the Third International Etty Hillesum Conference in Middelburg in 2018, reflected on this kneeling experience.[145] What made Etty's prayer so different, she said, was the surprise element. The urge to kneel always came without warning, which meant she had to kneel down on the spot, regardless of the circumstances. Sometimes it was in her room, either beside the little white table or by her bed. Other times it was somewhere else in the house, wherever she happened to be at that time. Once it happened in Dicky de Jonge's room where she suddenly knelt down "almost naked, in the middle of the floor, completely undone" by a desire to thank God.[146] Etty's kneeling was not a planned part of her day, but something that flowed from a sudden feeling of joy and gratitude.

This act of kneeling was so intimate that she had difficulty talking about it to anyone, even her lovers. On one occasion she knelt down in Han's room when he stepped out for something. When he unexpectedly returned and was taken aback at seeing her on the floor, she lied and told him she was just looking for a button.[147] With Julius Spier she was similarly shy. At one point she wanted to know if he knelt when he prayed, but she had difficulty framing the question. She finally brought it up casually while sewing a button for him, but then she lost her nerve and said no more. He pressed her to tell him what was on her mind, and she finally blurted it out: "Do you kneel as well?"[148] Apparently, he told her he did kneel, but she did not put that answer in her diary, saying instead "I still can't write about it."[149] From this conversation, as Clement points out, it appears that Etty did not get the idea of kneeling from Julius Spier. It was something she arrived at herself, but Spier did not discourage it because he was quietly doing the same thing.

And Julius Spier was not the only one influencing Etty Hillesum in this regard. We know that her friend Henny Tideman, who was a Christian, spoke freely about her habit of kneeling when she prayed.[150] Etty must have taken note of that. The writings of Rainer Maria Rilke may also have been an influence. Rilke said he prayed while kneeling, although he admitted that he was not sure whether the being to whom he turned was a deity or something else.[151] In any case, there was an important difference. For Tideman and Rilke, this kneeling was something intentional, something they decided to do before they began to pray. In Etty's case it was an unexpected urge that came from an inner space she called awe-inspiring.[152]

It was in that inner space that Etty Hillesum eventually developed a relationship with God that was personal and intimate. For her, God had become a friend—she addressed him as *You* (with a capital Y)—to whom she turned for comfort and protection:

"God, take me by Your hand, I shall follow You dutifully and not resist too much. I shall evade none of the tempests life has in store for me, I shall try to face it all as best I can."[153] A few months later she added: "I draw prayer around me like a dark protective wall, withdraw inside it as one might into a convent cell and then step outside again, calmer and stronger and more collected again. Withdrawing into the closed cell of prayer is becoming an ever-greater reality for me as well as a necessity."[154]

Such was the awe-inspiring God Etty found within herself as she lived through the cataclysmic events of World War II.

A Suffering God

In *The Brothers Karamazov*, Fyodor Dostoevsky deals with the immemorial question that philosophers and theologians call the problem of evil: how to reconcile the existence of a loving God with the existence of so much cruelty and evil in the world. It is one of the central questions in the novel, and Dostoevsky famously dramatizes it in Book V in a tavern conversation between two brothers who have very different views on religion: Ivan Karamazov, the doubter who despises all organized religion, and his young brother, Alyosha Karamazov, who is a novice in a Russian Orthodox monastery.

Ivan frames the problem by asking his monkish brother this question: Why does God allow so many innocent children in the world to suffer? Anticipating Alyosha's answer, he dismisses the idea that suffering can be seen as part of a divine plan for ultimate harmony in the universe. He renounces that kind of harmony, saying: "It's not worth the tears of that one tortured child."[155] If that is the price he has to pay to get into heaven, he says, he does not want to go there. "And so I give back my entrance ticket, and if I am an honest man I give it back as soon as possible," he says.[156]

Alyosha's response, not surprisingly, focuses on the Christian mystery of the cross. "But there is a Being and He can forgive everything, all and for all," he says, "because He gave His innocent blood for all and everything. You have forgotten Him, and on Him is built the edifice, and it is to Him they cry aloud: 'Thou are just, O Lord, for Thy ways are revealed!'"[157]

"Ah! The One without sin and His Blood!" Ivan responds. "No, I have not forgotten Him. On the contrary I've been wondering all the time how it was you did not bring Him in before, for usually all arguments on your side put Him in the foreground."[158]

Ivan goes on to tell his younger brother an ambiguous story about evil called "The Grand Inquisitor." According to this tale, Jesus comes back to earth and shows up in Seville Cathedral in Spain during the Inquisition. He performs many miracles there, even raising a little girl from the dead, and "the people are irresistibly drawn to him."[159] The result is that he is arrested on orders from the Grand Inquisitor and thrown into prison. The inquisitor eventually gives Jesus his freedom, but before letting him go he launches into a long monologue about the three temptations in the desert (when Jesus sparred with Satan). The point of the inquisitor's menacing monologue is to make a shocking claim: Throughout history, he says, the church has taken the side of Satan, and rightly so. The people have to eat, he says. What they want is food, not the interior freedom that Jesus claims to bring. In other words, the people want the stones turned into bread whether Jesus likes it or not. "Give bread, and man will worship thee, for nothing is more certain than bread," he says.[160] Throughout this entire diatribe, Jesus remains silent. In the end he goes over to the Grand Inquisitor, gives him a kiss, and leaves.

Dostoevsky's purpose in this conversation is to portray God as someone who chooses to be helpless in the face of human evil, someone who declines to use his power, instead taking suffering on himself for the salvation of humanity. And when Etty Hillesum brings up the problem of evil in her diary, she clearly has this conversation between the Karamazov brothers in mind. She specifically mentions Ivan's entrance ticket to heaven, but she does so in order to reject his conclusion. She has no intention of giving back *her* ticket, she writes, no matter what the cost. Yes, "the price of that admission ticket is high," she admits, "much blood and tears. But all the suffering and tears are worth it."[161]

Wil van den Bercken, who spoke at the 2008 Etty Hillesum Conference, made an important discovery for those of us who don't speak Dutch. In the English version of Etty's diary, he says, the words "admission ticket" are left out, thus significantly changing the meaning of the original Dutch and totally missing Etty's obvious allusion to *The Brothers Karamazov*. We are therefore using van den Bercken's own translation here.

Van den Bercken also highlights another significant example of Dostoevsky's influence in Etty's diary. It is found in the diary entry for 12 July 1942, in which Etty composes a prayer to God, but the God she addresses is the same "helpless" God that Dostoevsky talks about in "The Grand Inquisitor." Here is her prayer, in part:

> One thing is becoming increasingly clear to me: that You cannot help us, that we must help You to help ourselves. And that is all that we can manage these days and also all that really matters: that we safeguard that little piece of You, God, in ourselves. And perhaps in others as well. Alas, there doesn't seem to be much You Yourself can do about our circumstances, about our lives. Neither do I hold You responsible.[162]

For Etty Hillesum, then, the fact that God does not act against evil is not a reason to condemn him. Far from agreeing with Ivan Karamazov, she turns the tables on him. People like Ivan should begin by blaming themselves, she says. "God is not accountable to us, but we are to God," she writes. "I know what may lie in wait for us. Even now I am cut off from my parents and cannot reach them. . . . And yet I don't think life is meaningless. And God is not accountable to us for the senseless harm we cause one another. We are accountable to him."[163]

Father Zosima's View of Suffering

In addition to Alyosha Karamazov, Dostoevsky uses another character in *The Brothers Karamazov* to address the problem of evil. Father Zosima is a Russian Orthodox monk whose conversations and sermons take up all of Book VI; those conversations deal with the question of evil from a different angle, from the perspective of God's creation. For Father Zosima, there is a joy in creation despite the suffering and harsh realities of life. But to experience that joy, he says, we humans must take responsibility for the evil in the world and practice universal love despite that evil. We must be "a brother to everyone."[164] We are all guilty, he says, because we are all connected, but together we can change the world: "It's all like an ocean, I tell you. Then you would pray to the birds too, consumed by an all-embracing love, in a sort of transport, you would pray that they too would forgive you your sins. Treasure this ecstasy, however senseless it may seem to men."[165]

To illustrate this point, Father Zosima tells his hearers about his own youth when, as an officer in the army, he brutally mistreated an orderly under his command and later felt badly about it. But it was when he gazed on the beauty of nature that he truly realized how ugly his actions had been. "It was as though a sharp dagger had pierced me," he says. "I stood as in a trance, while the sun was shining, the leaves were rejoicing and the birds were trilling the praise of God. . . . I hid my face in my hands, fell on my bed and broke into a storm of tears."[166] In the presence of nature, the young Zosima felt moved to repent. He went to see the lowly soldier he mistreated, fell on his knees, and asked for forgiveness. "And there was such bliss in my heart as I have never known before in my life," he concludes.[167]

When Etty Hillesum describes life as "beautiful"—as she does countless times in her diary—she is reflecting this spirituality articulated by Father Zosima. The kinship between the two is remarkable, as Wil van den Bercken points out.[168] In an entry in September 1942, for example, she mentions her oft-repeated ambition to be a writer with a mission, and the most important part of that mission is to find "the words that proclaim how good and beautiful it is to live in Your world, oh God, despite everything we human beings do to one another."[169] Etty is contrasting the evil of people's deeds with the beauty of creation, just as Zosima does, and her descriptions of creation's beauty are as lyrical as Zosima's. While Zosima sees God in the shimmering leaves, the singing birds, and the noble horse, she sees God in the silvery moon, the jasmine behind her house, and the cornfields of Deventer "whose beauty nearly brought me to my knees."[170] And like Father Zosima, it is this beauty in creation that leads her to have an all-embracing love and forgiveness for all of humanity, and an acceptance of personal responsibility for the evil in the world. "All disasters stem from us," she writes. "Why is there war? Perhaps because now and then I might be inclined to snap at my neighbor. Because I and my neighbor and everyone else do not have enough love. Yet we could fight war and all its excrescences by releasing, each day, the love that is shackled inside us and giving it a chance to live."[171]

This way of looking at the problem of evil, as van den Bercken points out, is not intellectually satisfying for people who don't personally believe in God.[172] It is not the clear-cut answer that secular intellectuals want. It is only acceptable to somebody who is comfortable with mystery, somebody who is able to let faith coexist with unresolved questions. Dostoevsky was one such believer, and Etty Hillesum became one. She did not need a black-and-white answer to every question. She was able to live with the ambiguity she found in "The Grand Inquisitor." "You have placed me before Your ultimate mysteries, oh God," she writes in her last notebook. "I am grateful to You for that, I even have the strength to accept it and to know there is no answer. That we must be able to bear Your mysteries."[173]

Van den Bercken's final remarks to the 2008 conference provide a fitting conclusion to this chapter:

> Nowhere does Etty Hillesum give a systematic description of her relationship to, or opinion of, *The Brothers Karamazov*. However, the similarity in religious spirituality between Hillesum's diary and Dostoyevsky's last novel is striking and, given her interest in Dostoyevsky, no accident. One can read Etty Hillesum's reflections as an echo of Dostoyevsky.[174]

Chapter 4

Joy in a Nazi Camp: An Atypical Mystic

"Sometimes when I stand in some corner of the camp, my feet planted on Your earth, my eyes turned toward Your heaven, tears sometimes run down my face, tears of deep emotion and gratitude," Etty Hillesum wrote while in Westerbork transit camp. "At night too, when I lie in my bed and rest in you, oh God, tears of gratitude run down my face, and that is my prayer."[175]

Those are unusual words. Not many prisoners, living in the filth and misery of Westerbork, could look heavenward and feel sentiments of joy and gratitude rather than tears of bitterness and fear. Or take a walk by the barbed wire at night and, rather than notice the menacing watch towers and armed guards, gaze in wonderment at a full moon "made of silver and eternity: like a plaything that had slipped from God's preoccupied hand."[176]

Where were those feelings of joy and gratitude coming from? Certainly not from Etty's reasoning—logic had nothing to do with it. Nor from some state of hallucination—nobody was more rooted in reality than she was. Those feelings were coming from deep within her, from the ground of her soul, from that part of her that was made in the image and likeness of God. She said as much herself. Time and again, she wrote, "It soars straight from the heart—I can't help it, that's just the way it is, like some elemental force."[177] We Christians see that experience of God as the work of the Holy Spirit, and that seems to be the case here.

The Holy Spirit had penetrated her soul. Expressions of such joy and gratitude are usually signs of the Holy Spirit, as St. Paul reminds us in his Letter to the Galatians.[178]

In this case, the Holy Spirit used the particular circumstances of her life as the instrument for divine action. The horror of concentration camps was the "fodder used by the Holy Spirit" to illuminate Etty's path and bring her to an understanding of herself and of God, as Sr. Jean Marie points out in her book *The Unfolding Journey*.[179] In other words, Etty found holiness *through* the Holocaust, not *despite* it, by baring her breast to it rather than running away from it. It was in that struggle that she became a mystic. But she was a different sort of mystic. Her writing never reached the spiritual depths of the great saints like Teresa of Ávila and John of the Cross. Hers was not the mysticism of someone who prayed for hours in the stillness of a convent chapel, away from the pressures and fears of the world. Her spirituality was born in the crucible of Nazi hate, and it reflected the struggle she waged to make sense of that horror. Nazi camps became the instrument of her holiness.

Professor Francesca Brezzi, an expert on the philosophy of gender at the University of Rome, sums it up this way: Etty's was a "mysticism which is not stillness, but a profound, thirsty restlessness that impels one to search again and again. It is a feeling that awakens and does not look for ecstatic experiences, but a meeting, a union with what life really reveals and demands of us."[180] Etty herself put it this way:

> Living and dying, sorrow and joy, the blisters on my feet and the jasmine behind the house, the persecution, the unspeakable horrors—it is all one in me, and I accept it all as one mighty whole and begin to grasp it better if only for myself. . . . Yes, we carry everything within us,

God and Heaven and Hell and Earth and Life and Death and all of history.[181]

Notice that Etty is speaking here of that "outer space within" which she referred to as *Weltinnenraum* (a German word she picked up from Rilke). That was also part of her mysticism. For her the inner world encompassed everything the outer world encompassed, including suffering. Especially suffering![182] Etty had a gift for feeling the pain of others: "I experience people, and I also experience the suffering of people," she wrote in June 1942.[183]

The Search for Meaning

In chapter 2 we looked at Etty's struggle to deal with her emotional chaos, and in chapter 3 we described her search for God. But beneath all of that restlessness was the search for meaning or purpose in life. That was how her path to God began. That was the fodder that the Holy Spirit used to bring her along. Etty mentions that search again and again in her diary, beginning with the first page of the first entry, on 9 March 1941, where she says that giving her life a "reasonable and satisfactory purpose" is why she is writing this diary in the first place.[184] Some twenty months later, while describing the horrors of Westerbork, she was saying the same thing in more forceful terms: "Yet if we have nothing to offer a desolate post-war world but our bodies saved at any cost, if we fail to draw new meaning from the deep wells of our distress and despair, then it will not be enough."[185] Sometimes this search for meaning came when she was feeling depressed, or had heard about more arrests of neighbors she knew well. At other times it came when she was feeling more optimistic. But whatever the occasion, finding "meaning and beauty" in life was paramount, as was the hope that in the end "we have realized our potential and lived a good life."[186]

A key to this search for meaning was her ability to see the big picture, the flow of history—what philosophers call seeing *sub specie aeternitatis*. One afternoon Etty found herself walking with a blister on her foot and overcome with tiredness, but she was not allowed to take a train or sit down at one of the many pavement cafés. Such were the regulations that harassed Jews every time they went outside the door. But rather than being overcome with anger at this injustice, a liberating thought "welled up" inside her. "I am not alone in my tiredness or sickness or fears," she wrote, "but one with millions of others from many centuries, and it is all part of life, and yet life is beautiful and meaningful too. It is meaningful even in its meaninglessness."[187]

> How can it be [she said about Westerbork] that this stretch of heathland surrounded by barbed wire, through which so much human misery had flooded, nevertheless remains inscribed in my memory as something almost lovely? How is it that my spirit, far from being oppressed, seemed to grow lighter and brighter there? It is because I read the signs of the times, and they did not seem meaningless to me. Surrounded by my writers and poets and the flowers on my desk, I loved life.[188]

Even the flowers on her desk hinted at this deeper meaning to life. Etty loved flowers, all flowers: the magnolia in the corner of Tideman's room "whose mysterious beauty almost scared me stiff"; the sweet peas she picked up while out on a walk whose colors were so subtle that words failed her; the jasmine at the back of her house that made her want "to believe in miracles in the twentieth century."[189] For her, these flowers were proof that life was indeed beautiful despite the horrors around her. She also loved the two gaunt trees outside her window. One night in the spring of 1942 she went to bed early and found herself gazing out the window at those trees:

> And it was once more as if life with all its mysteries was close to me, as if I could touch it. I had the feeling that I was resting against the naked breast of life, and could feel her gentle and regular heartbeat. I felt safe and protected. And I thought, How strange. It is wartime. There are concentration camps. Small barbarity upon small barbarity.[190]

That night, Etty's dreamy thoughts had moved from the ascetic beauty of the two trees, to the stark horror of the Nazis, to the feeling that she was protected by God and that there was meaning in it all despite the barbarity. She had her fingertips on the contours of history, and she saw that it had meaning.

But there is more. Etty also saw suffering as meaningful, even redemptive. For her, suffering was something that humanizes us and gives our lives a deeper significance. There are clear echoes here of Fyodor Dostoevsky, but she also drew from German and French writers such as Karl Nötzel, Walter Schubart, and André Suarès, who wrote extensively about the Russian people's ability to suffer. Etty liked those writers, despite their tendency to over-romanticize Russia. People in the West, she said, like to have theories and philosophies to explain everything, and in the process they "do not endure and experience, bear and suffer to the full."[191] Russians don't have to intellectualize everything in that way, according to Etty. They simply accept suffering with meekness and humility.[192] "I do not claim that we must look upon pain as perfection," she wrote, quoting André Suarès. "Indeed, we must do all we can to rid ourselves of it. But we must be acquainted with pain. Real man is neither master of his pain, nor a fugitive from it, nor its slave: he must be pain's redeemer."[193]

In addition to her study of the Russian soul, Etty learned from her personal experience in therapy. It was Julius Spier who taught her to accept the pain of her own childhood and integrate it into her adult life. That lesson gave her the deep and abiding conviction that suffering must never be allowed to develop into a destructive force in one's life, as it had in the lives of many she knew. "We are here to take some of the world's suffering upon ourselves by baring our breast to it, not to increase it by our violence," she wrote.[194]

In these entries, Etty Hillesum was articulating a theology of the cross without using theological language, and she did it with more clarity than many Christians could. Most people, even those of us who believe in the redemptive power of the cross, find suffering difficult to accept. The cross is, as St. Paul said, a stumbling block to the Jews and a scandal to the Gentiles. And if it is difficult for us in our ordinary uneventful lives, how much more difficult would it be if we found ourselves in a world of concentration camps and death. Novelist François Mauriac expresses this well in the foreword he wrote for Elie Wiesel's book *Night*, in which he describes his helplessness when he met Wiesel for the first time and discovered that he was a Holocaust survivor. As a practicing Catholic, Mauriac's own views on suffering were well defined and deeply rooted in the theology of the cross. For him, God was a God of love whose death on the cross gave meaning to all human suffering in every age and in every situation, no matter how horrific. But when he tried to explain that to Wiesel, who had suffered the atrocities of Auschwitz and Buchenwald, words failed him. In the foreword, Mauriac writes:

What did I say to him? Did I speak to him of that other Jew, this crucified brother who perhaps resembled him and whose cross conquered the world? Did I explain to him that what had been a stumbling block for *his* faith had become a cornerstone for *mine*? And that the connection between the cross and human suffering remains, in my view, the key to the unfathomable mystery in which the faith of his childhood was lost?[195]

Faced with a real-life survivor of the Holocaust, Mauriac couldn't get the words out. All he could do was embrace his new friend and weep.

Mauriac's words describe how most of us would feel in the presence of a Holocaust survivor. Even if that survivor were Etty Hillesum, our reaction might not be very different—except for one thing. With Etty, it might be easier to broach the question of the cross. She was not a baptized Christian, but she did see suffering as redemptive.

A Refusal to Hate

On 29 September 1941, Etty wrote in her diary about the need to "stop for a while to take stock" of her life.[196] She wanted to organize her life better and to take better care of her physical and mental health, adding "right now, sunning myself this Monday morning in the sun lounge, wearing my Japanese dressing gown, it feels as if everything is too much for me and I find myself unable to get down to work."[197]

Etty was feeling frustrated that she wasn't getting enough studying and writing done. There were too many distractions. Later that day, she gave a specific example of what she meant by a distraction, a specific person whom she referred to as "that damned Aleida." Clearly Etty wasn't happy with this Aleida, because several days later she was still annoyed, commenting: "Her voice still shrills in my ear when I think of it."[198]

This is what happened. The previous Friday, Etty had a discussion with Aleida about the Nazi program of extermination in Holland and how Jews were coping with it. In the course of the conversation, Etty said that she did not share the hate that so many Jews and others felt for the occupiers. She could not live with that kind of anger in her heart, she said. Not surprisingly, Aleida disagreed. All eighty million Germans should be exterminated, she said. Not a single one should be left alive! "Oh, I just gloat when I stand by the window at night and hear the (Allied) planes overhead," she said.[199] Now it was Etty's turn to become angry—not at the Germans, but at Aleida and her attitude. Apparently she didn't mince her words, because several days later she was still fuming at her friend: "And it was as if her bosom was heaving and her nostrils flaring, although she has no bosom to speak of and a silly little nose."[200] (Etty wasn't above hurling a personal insult when she felt like it!)

Etty broke one of her own rules that day. She and Julius Spier had often talked about the fact that they didn't hate the Nazis, but they agreed not to say that openly in company because no one would understand.[201] She had been open about her feelings with Aleida, and sure enough Aleida didn't understand. Later that same day she made the same mistake again, this time with Bernard, a fellow boarder in the house where she lived. As soon as she got home, she burst into Bernard's room uninvited (he had a friend visiting him) and asked them point-blank: "Tell me do you also think that every last German ought to be exterminated," to which Bernard and his friend answered yes. Etty again expressed her strong disapproval of that attitude, and "a furious and passionate discussion ensued." All told, it was a stormy day for Etty, but she had no regrets. "One could write a whole pamphlet on that one evening," she wrote in the diary.[202]

Etty Hillesum did not react to the Holocaust in the way most people did. It was not in her nature. "I cannot hate any-one," she said.[203] Not that she didn't have her own moments of anger. "Sometimes when I read the papers or hear reports of what is happening all round, I am suddenly beside myself with anger, cursing and swearing at the Germans," she wrote in March 1941.[204] But then she would stop herself and make a resolution to love her enemies, even the Nazis. One of her supporters in this was Spier, who shared her sentiments. "If there were only one human being worthy of the name of 'man,' then we should be justified in believing in men and humanity," he said to her one day. She was so happy to hear those words that she threw her arms around him.[205]

"It is the problem of our age: hatred of Germans poisons everyone's mind," she wrote. "Let the bastards drown, the lot of them—such sentiments have become part and parcel of our daily speech and sometimes makes one feel that life these days has become impossible."[206]

Several months later, on 25 February 1942, Etty gives us another example of her refusal to hate. Spier, as a legal immigrant from Germany, had to fill out some forms at the Gestapo offices in Amsterdam and Etty decided to go with him for support. A large group of Jews was crowded into the hall that morning, but she found the officers to be surprisingly civilized. "We entered a nice warm room and were received very correctly by very correct gentlemen wearing all sorts of insignia," she wrote, "and we ourselves were very correct as well. We politely signed the papers they politely slid across to us, which could well have been our death-warrants."[207] What Etty saw that morning was a system that had engulfed everyone, the men behind the desks and those being questioned alike. The Gestapo officers had no choice but to play along whether they agreed with the program or not, she thought.

But in the hall that morning, Etty noticed a young Gestapo who was not as friendly as the others. He was pacing up and down with a sullen expression on his face, and he made no attempt to hide his dislike for the Jews in the hall. He kept looking for pretexts to shout at his helpless victims, yelling things like: "Take your hands out of your pockets." Let Etty herself describe what happened next:

> When it was my turn to stand in front of his desk, he bawled at me: "What the hell's so funny?"
>
> I wanted to say: "Nothing's funny here except you," but refrained.
>
> "You're still smirking," he bawled again.
>
> And I in all innocence: "I didn't mean to, it's just my usual expression."
>
> And he: "Don't give me that, get the hell out of here," his face saying "I'll deal with you later."
>
> And that was presumably meant to scare me to death, but the device was too transparent.[208]

Etty wasn't angry at that officer. She felt sorry for him because she saw him as somebody trapped in a political system, caught in "an ominous structure capable of crashing down on all of us, on top of the interrogators and on the interrogated."[209] What needed eradicating was the evil in man, not man himself, she wrote. For Etty, this pacifism extended to the entire war; she didn't share the wish of so many Jews that the Allies would obliterate Germany. "I often wonder why this war and everything connected with it afflicts me so little," she wrote on 14 December 1941. "Perhaps because it is my second great war? I was in the thick of the first, and then relived it all in the postwar literature. So much rebelliousness, so much hatred, the passion, the arguments, the call for social justice, the class struggle, etc. We have been through it all. To go through it a second time just won't do—it becomes a cliché."[210]

Etty was deeply suspicious of the political ideologies of her day—Marxism, fascism, socialism, any -ism. "Socialism lets in hatred against everything that is not socialist through the back door," she wrote.[211] It may be for this reason that she broke up with her old boyfriend, Klaas Smelik, although they remained friends till the end of her life. Smelik was an old Trotskyite, a radical who wanted to upend social structures in the name of social justice. Etty's problem with that ideology was the hidden agenda of hate: its success depended on inciting hate between the classes in society. The upper class was the enemy. She wrote in her diary:

> Klaas, all I really wanted to say is this. We have so much work to do on ourselves that we shouldn't even be thinking of hating our so-called enemies. We are hurtful to one another as it is. . . . Each of us must turn inward and destroy in himself all that he thinks he ought to destroy in others. And remember that every atom of hate we add to this world makes it still more inhospitable. And you, Klaas, dogged old class fighter that you have always been, dismayed and astonished at the same time, say, "But that—that is nothing but Christianity." And I, amused by your confusion, retort quite coolly, "Yes, Christianity, and why ever not?"[212]

An Attraction to Christianity

When Etty said we must begin by changing the evil within ourselves, she was articulating what we Christians call the doctrine of Original Sin, something she must have known about from her reading of St. Augustine, Meister Eckhart, and others. That doctrine (based in the book of Genesis) explains that we are all fallen human beings, all sinners, all responsible in some way for the hatred in the world. Etty was familiar with that idea even though she was not baptized herself. As well as picking it up from her favorite writers, she learned about it from her Jewish mentor, Julius Spier. Spier once told her that he had a dream that Christ himself came to baptize him, and it is significant that Etty remembered that detail when she wrote about Spier after his death.[213] Though he never sought baptism that we know of, Spier read the New Testament and was attracted to Christ. And we know that Etty loved the New Testament, especially the Gospel of Matthew, and must have felt attracted to Christ also. The God that she eventually discovered within herself was the God of the Bible, the God of St. Augustine and Fyodor Dostoevsky and Meister Eckhart.

"It can honestly be said that Etty Hillesum not only does not criticize Christianity, but manifests a spontaneous sympathy for it as far as she perceives it," says Fr. Paul Lebeau, S.J., who spoke at the 2008 Etty Hillesum Conference. "It is thus self-evident that numerous Christian readers from different backgrounds feel challenged and comforted in their belief, in their relation to God and men, by the authenticity of the testimony that she bears in her writings, her life and her confrontation with death."[214]

Her Struggle to Overcome Jealousy

The words Julius Spier chose for his tombstone were words that Etty might well have chosen for hers if she could have. They come from St. Paul's First Letter to the Corinthians: "Now remains

Faith, Hope, Love, these three. But the greatest of these is Love."[215] Those words were life-giving for Etty when she was going through a fit of jealousy over Spier's fiancée, Hertha. After reading some love letters Hertha had sent to Spier, Etty was unhappy, and she immediately opened the epistles of St. Paul for solace. The passage her eyes fell upon was that same passage that Spier liked, and the effect the words had on her was so profound that she had difficulty describing it. "They worked on me like a divining rod that touched the bottom of my heart, causing hidden sources to spring up suddenly within me," she wrote. "All at once I was down on my knees beside the little white table and all my released love coursed through me again, purged of desire, envy, spite, etc."[216]

Etty never forgot that experience. Ten months later, in a letter she wrote to friends in The Hague, she called attention to that passage: "And I also believe, childishly perhaps but stubbornly, that the earth will become more hospitable again only through the love that the Jew Paul described to the citizens of Corinth in the thirteenth chapter of his first letter."[217]

Important as Paul's letter was to Etty, the Gospel of Matthew eventually became even more so. She quoted from that Gospel frequently in the later parts of her diary, and one quotation in particular is worth noting because it was written at a difficult time in her life, right after Spier's death. At that time, she found herself quoting the following words in her diary: "Therefore if thou bring thy gift to the altar, and there remember that thy brother hath aught against thee; leave there thy gift before the altar, and go thy way; first be reconciled to thy brother, and then come and offer thy gift."[218] Ria van den Brandt, a Dutch scholar and one of the speakers at the 2018 Etty Hillesum Conference, points out that if you look closely at her original diary (which is now in the Jewish Historical Museum in Amsterdam), you will notice that part of the quotation is underlined: Etty underlined the phrases "and there remember that thy brother hath aught against thee," and "first be reconciled to thy brother."[219] Shortly afterward, she quoted it again, this time in *The Art of Living: Thoughts from Week to Week*, the calendar she and Henny Tideman were keeping together. (The year-long calendar had a quotation from a famous author on each right-hand page and a blank space on the left-hand side where the reader was invited to write in a favorite quotation that would match.)

Van den Brandt surmises that there was a reason this quotation about forgiveness was so important to Etty at this time. Etty had been competing with Henny for Spier's affections and had gone through phases of jealousy over it. But after Spier's death—which is when she and Henny began keeping that calendar—her friendship with Henny became closer as her feelings of jealousy began to recede. Etty's decision to copy Matthew's "love for enemies" and other texts from the Sermon on the Mount may have been determined by her desire to reconcile with Henny, van den Brandt says: "Perhaps she chose to honor Spier after his death by using the texts she had read together with him and Tideman."[220]

A Refusal to Fear

If Etty's refusal to hate made her unusual, so did her refusal to fear. That was apparent the morning she went with Spier to fill out forms at the Gestapo office. The officer who was yelling at everybody that morning didn't scare her. She felt sorry for him. But her deepest compassion was reserved for the inmates she saw at Westerbork transit camp, victims who were trapped by fear, trapped by what she called "the thousand petty anxieties."[221] She wrote of her Westerbork experience:

At night, as I lay in the camp on my plank bed surrounded by women and girls, gently snoring, dreaming aloud, quietly sobbing, tossing and turning, women and girls who often told me during the day, "We don't want to think, we don't want to feel, otherwise we are sure to go out of our minds," I was sometimes filled with an infinite tenderness, and lay awake for hours letting all the many, too many impressions of a much-too-long-day wash over me, and I prayed, "Let me be the thinking heart of these barracks." And that is what I want to be again. The thinking heart of a whole concentration camp.[222]

Etty did indeed become the thinking heart of the whole camp, and fearlessness was part of her heart. She was fearless in the face of Nazi harassment, but also fearless in the face of death—including her own. By this time Etty had let go of any hopes she might have had that the Allies would free her people from the Nazis. "What is at stake is our impending destruction and annihilation, we can have no more illusions about that," she wrote on 3 July 1942. "They are out to destroy us completely, we must accept that and go on from there."[223] Then she added these startling words:

I have looked our destruction, our miserable end, which has already begun in so many small ways in our daily lives, straight in the eye and accepted it into my life and my love of life has not been diminished. I am not bitter or rebellious or in any way discouraged. I continue to grow from day to day, even with the likelihood of destruction staring me in the face.[224]

Rainer Maria Rilke's verses on death, some of which she quotes in her diary, helped Etty achieve this remarkable detachment.[225] Under his influence she saw death as "an old acquaintance," something to be accepted as a natural part of life. She refused to waste her energies worrying about it. "Through non-acceptance and through having all those fears, most people are left with just a pitiful and mutilated slice of life, which can hardly be called life at all," she wrote. "It sounds paradoxical: by excluding death from our life, we cannot live a full life, and by admitting death into our life we enlarge and enrich it."[226] Etty Hillesum wrote those wise words at the tender age of 28.

Her Sexuality Transformed

In his encyclical *Deus Caritas Est*, Pope Benedict XVI reminds us that the reason we humans love God is that God loved us first. The initiative came from God, not from us. "We have come to know and to believe in the love God has for us," he writes, quoting from the First Letter of John. "In these words the Christian can express the fundamental decision of his life. Being Christian is not the result of an ethical choice or a lofty idea, but the encounter with an event, a person, which gives life a new horizon and a decisive direction."[227]

The purpose of the encyclical, the pope says, is to reflect on this love which God mysteriously and gratuitously offers to humans, and to underline "the intrinsic link between that Love and the reality of human love."[228] The pope goes on to examine two words for human love that the ancient Greeks used: *eros* and *agape*. *Eros* was the word for sexual love between man and woman, and *agape* the word for self-sacrificing love. Sometimes these two forms of love are wrongly seen as opposed to each other, the pope says, with *eros* being viewed as self-serving and corrupting, and *agape* being viewed as the only true form of love. Many critics blame the Church for this, the pope observes. They claim that Christianity poisoned the gift of *eros* in the course of history with too many rules and regulations, casting what should be an ecstatic (even divine) experience in a negative light, full of guilt. Pope Benedict roundly rejects that criticism. What Christianity opposed was not the joy of *eros*, he says, but a warped and destructive form of it, one that pretended to portray sexual love as divinely inspired while in reality debasing it. As an example, he cites the "sacred" prostitution cults practiced at the temples of the ancient Greeks:

> The Greeks—not unlike other cultures—considered *eros* principally as a kind of intoxication, the overpowering of reason by a "divine madness" which tears man away from his finite existence and enables him, in the very process of being overwhelmed by divine power, to experience supreme happiness. All other powers in heaven and earth appear secondary. . . . *Eros* was thus celebrated as divine power, as fellowship with the Divine.[229]

But was this cult really fellowship with the Divine, as the Greeks claimed? Pope Benedict's answer is no. What the Greeks were doing in those ancient temples, he writes, far from achieving fellowship with the Divine, stripped *eros* of its dignity and actually dehumanized it. He calls it a counterfeit divinization of *eros*: "Indeed, the prostitutes in the temple, who had to bestow this divine intoxication, were not treated as human beings and persons, but simply used as a means of arousing 'divine madness.'" They were not goddesses but victims of exploitation, he says, young women who were abused by a warped and destructive form of love. "An intoxicated and undisciplined *eros*, then, is not an ascent in 'ecstasy' towards the Divine, but a fall, a degradation of man," he concludes.[230]

Pope Benedict gives this example to make a point about the beauty and sacredness of sexual love, properly understood. There is indeed a certain relationship between *eros* and the Divine, he says, but we need to be careful. If *eros* is to be a genuine "foretaste of the pinnacle of our existence" and not just a passing selfish pleasure, it must be transformed by self-sacrifice:

> Love promises infinity, eternity—a reality far greater and totally other than our everyday existence. Yet we have also seen that the way to attain this goal is not simply by submitting to instinct. Purification and growth in maturity are called for; and these also pass through the path of renunciation. Far from rejecting or "poisoning" *eros*, they heal and restore its true grandeur.[231]

Love is indeed ecstasy, the pope says, "not in the sense of a moment of intoxication, but rather as a journey, an ongoing exodus out of the closed inward-looking self towards its liberation through self-giving, and thus towards authentic self-discovery and indeed the discovery of God."[232]

Which brings us back to Etty Hillesum. Sexual liberation was one of the paths Etty travelled on her way to discovering God. In her particular case, it can be said that the joy of sexual love did indeed lead to the Divine. This point was clearly articulated by Catholic theologian Maria Clara Lucchetti Bingemer at the Etty Hillesum Conference in 2014.[233] Paradoxical as it may sound, Bingemer said, Etty's life demonstrates an important side of authentic Christian love, although she was not a Christian herself. She was "a young, beautiful and very sexy woman," Bingemer said, "someone well aware of her body and her sexual appetites."[234] But at the same time, sexual love became for Etty, not something selfish, connected only to sex, but something that included care and concern for the beloved, even to the point of self-giving and sacrifice. Hers was an example of how to integrate *eros* and *agape*. The catalyst for this radical liberation was undoubtedly Julius Spier, Bingemer said. He was simultaneously her lover and mystagogue: "Through Spier, she came to see how suffering, when accepted, does not diminish, but qualitatively strengthens life. Love between them was at the same time erotic and contemplative."[235]

Bingemer notes a high point in Etty's spiritual journey (30 April 1942) when she began to see her relationship with Spier in a new light. Something had matured within her by that time, something that enabled her to make a most unusual decision. She decided to marry Spier, but not in the way most people understand marital commitment. It would be a "pretend marriage" devoid of all possessiveness, a relationship with just one purpose in mind; to be by Spier's side if he were ever deported by the Nazis. "One day I would surrender him unharmed to his girlfriend," she added.[236] (She was referring to Hertha Levi, Spier's fiancée in London.) Says Bingemer: "Etty Hillesum's love for Julius Spier, as passionate as it was in the beginning, did not belong exclusively to *eros*. It evolved into an inclusive love, even as it remained particular and singular, a woman who loved a man in all the fullness that loving can entail."[237] For that reason, her writings are of great importance, Bingemer says, "in demonstrating that agapic joy, the enjoyment of the soul, is not incompatible with the pleasures of the body and sex. On the contrary, *eros* figures in and can even be a route to a relationship with God and also an intimation of the indescribable flights of mystical experience."[238]

As it turned out, Spier died on 15 September 1942, four and a half months after Etty made the decision to "marry" him. By then, Etty's love (*agape*) had led her to volunteer as a social worker in Westerbork transit camp, to console the victims of deportation there and be "a balm for all wounds."[239] She also used a surprising image to express this *agape*—surprising simply because she was not Catholic. "I have broken my body like bread and shared it among men," she wrote. "And why not, they were hungry and had gone without for so long."[240] Whether this reference to the Eucharist was deliberate or unconscious on Etty's part we can't say.

What we can say is that Etty Hillesum was a mystic, although not a traditionally Catholic one. We Catholics should not try to "canonize" her or turn her into one of our own, but we can see the action of the Holy Spirit in her remarkable life nonetheless.[241] As Bingemer says, "Etty Hillesum is heiress to the mystical tradition that is born of the Spirit that moves freely anywhere and in anyone, a tradition that belongs to the whole of humankind, itself finite but inhabited by the Infinite."[242]

"We Left the Camp Singing"

When Etty Hillesum's time for deportation came on 7 September 1943, it was a shock, "a body blow" that struck her down because she wasn't expecting it.[243] She knew that her parents could be transported any day, but she assumed that her status with the Jewish Council protected her—for the present at least. That assumption might have been correct were it not for something unwise that her mother did. Riva wrote a letter to Johann Baptist Albin Rauter, the head of the SS in the Netherlands, requesting more freedom of movement for her family because of Mischa's standing as a talented pianist. Families with gifted children were sometimes given such exemptions, and Riva thought writing a letter was worth a try.

She was wrong. Rauter's fanatical hatred of Jews was legendary, even among his own colleagues. He was, as some observers said, "the incarnation of the Aryan hero, whose fingers would be besmirched by touching the paper of this letter."[244] Having the impertinence to write a letter to any high-ranking Nazi officer was risky, but writing to a personage such as Commander Rauter, a confidant of Heinrich Himmler, was unthinkable. True to form, he was enraged at the arrival of this letter from a Jew and sent a telegram to Westerbork ordering the immediate deportation of the pianist Mischa Hillesum and his family to Auschwitz. The telegram arrived late on Monday night, after the train had been filled, but the camp commandant, A. K. Gemmeker, wanted the order carried out anyway.

Friends of the Hillesum family immediately got busy packing food and clothes into three rucksacks: one for Mischa, one for his father, and one for his mother. Nobody thought to include Etty because everyone assumed she had special status. But then word came down that Etty had to go also. Friends immediately appealed to Kurt Schlesinger, a Jew who had influence with the commandant, but they were told that there was no hope. Gemmeker had interpreted the order from headquarters as including Etty, and there was no way of changing his mind, Schlesinger said. None![245]

Jopie Vleeschhouwer, who had become a friend of Etty's in Westerbork—they took walks together at night along the barbed wire—wrote a letter to Etty's friends in Amsterdam describing Etty's departure on that fateful Tuesday morning, 7 September 1943. The letter is filled with a palpable sadness. Etty's father relieved his nerves by making humorous jokes, Vleeschhouwer wrote, which irritated Mischa because his father was not taking the situation seriously enough. But what upset Mischa most was having to leave all his music behind. "I managed to squeeze four scores into his rucksack," Vleeschhouwer wrote.[246] The rest were sent back to Amsterdam in a suitcase. As for Etty, she was her usual radiant self after she recovered from her initial shock. Here is Vleeschhouwer's description of her:

> Talking gaily, smiling, a kind word for everyone she met on the way, full of sparkling good humor, perhaps just a touch of sadness, but every inch our Etty, the way you all know her. "I have my diaries and my small Bibles, and my Russian grammar and Tolstoy with me, and I have no idea what else there is in my luggage."[247]

Etty ended up in wagon 12 of the train, and her parents and brother in wagon 1. As the train moved away, what imprinted itself on Vleeschhouwer's memory was the "swift glimpse of Mischa's waving hand through a chink in Wagon Number 1, then a cheerful 'byeee' from Etty in 12, and . . . they were gone."[248] It was a hard day for a great many people, he wrote, and "the way they felt about her leaving spoke volumes for the love and dedication she had given to all."[249]

As we saw, the last written words from Etty Hillesum that we know of come from a postcard that a farmer found that day in one of his fields next to a railroad track in the northeastern Netherlands. Thankfully, the farmer suspected that the postcard had been thrown from a Nazi train and he took the trouble to drop it in the mail. (Today it is preserved in the Jewish Historical Museum in Amsterdam.) The postcard is addressed to Christine van Nooten, the teacher who had an affair with Etty's father. This is what it says:

> Christine, opening the Bible at random I find this: "The Lord is my high tower."[250] I am sitting on my rucksack in the middle of a full freight car. Father, Mother,

and Mischa are a few cars away. In the end, the departure came without warning. On sudden special orders from The Hague. We left the camp singing, Father and Mother firmly and calmly, Mischa, too. We shall be travelling for three days. Thank you for all your kindness and care. Friends left behind will still be writing to Amsterdam; perhaps you will hear something from them. Or from my last long letter from camp.

Good-bye for now from the four of us.

Etty[251]

Chapter 5

A Train Ride into Hell: Edith Stein's Story

Before we witness the final chapter of Etty Hillesum's life, we need to pause and introduce another mystic to our story. St. Edith Stein was in many ways very different from Etty Hillesum, with a different background and history, but like Etty she struggled to make sense of the horrors of World War II, and like Etty she was murdered in Auschwitz-Birkenau. Comparing the two women is irresistible because the road that Edith took to God in many ways resembles Etty's road.

In this chapter we will follow that road, a journey that began in Germany and eventually led to Holland where Edith's path briefly crossed that of Etty in Westerbork in 1942. We will suggest that these two intellectuals have more in common than they have to divide them, especially when it comes to the crucial questions of suffering and death. As mentioned in the introduction, we do not know to what extent they were able to communicate during the four days Edith Stein was in Westerbork, but they share the brutality of their common destiny. As Fr. Paul Lebeau, S.J., puts it: "Forever connected by the same tragic fate, about which their writings bear witness—their sense of the Absolute, their experience of prayer, their broad culture, the depth and the relevance of their ideas regarding the ultimate questions—all that allows us to imagine that they would have happily entered into dialogue and friendship in this life."[252]

Edith Stein was born on 12 October 1891 in Breslau, a large city in what was then Germany; after World War II it became Wrocław, Poland. She was the youngest of eleven children and grew up in a prominent well-to-do Orthodox Jewish family of Prussian nationality, where synagogue services were at the center of life. At the age of nineteen she entered the University of Breslau and signed up for some basic courses with a teaching career in mind, but she also took some lectures in psychology. Although by then she had stopped practicing her faith or praying in any form, she was haunted by questions about human existence: Do human beings have an immortal soul? What is the structure of the human person? Edith hoped for answers to those questions in her psychology class, but the more she heard the more disillusioned she became. Far from dealing seriously with the question of a soul, the lectures she attended were explaining it away.

"She found herself confronted with a quantitative approach based on the methods of the natural sciences, determined to prove that the soul she was investigating did not exist at all," says biographer Waltraud Herbstrith. "The entire notion of the soul had been relegated to the realm of the irrational and mythological, henceforth to be regarded with a skeptical smile."[253] Edith Stein was deeply dissatisfied with that answer.

What is truth?

At this point, a famous philosopher came to Edith's rescue. In her reading she came upon the writings of Professor Edmund Husserl (1859–1938), a Jewish-turned-Lutheran philosopher who was considered the founder of a new movement in Europe called phenomenology. Husserl's reasoning immediately fascinated Edith because it was so different from the intellectual mainstream in which she found herself. Most philosophers of her day were followers of Immanuel Kant and the European Enlightenment, intellectuals who saw truth as purely subjective. In other words, each person must give his or her own meaning to things; religion and the existence of God, they said, are a matter of how one feels, not a matter of objective truth. Husserl and the phenomenologists were now challenging that philosophy, saying that if one takes off the rationalistic blinders of natural science, one can discover a reality that is objective and perennial. In effect, these phenomenologists were rediscovering the insights of medieval scholasticism, which had insisted centuries earlier that a Divine Creator does really exist, independent of the human mind, and that belief in that Creator is completely compatible with human reason.

Edith Stein was excited. She left Breslau and went to the university in Göttingen where Husserl was teaching, and immediately became part of a group of young intellectuals who had gathered around the phenomenologist. She took to this new movement like a fish to water, eventually becoming Husserl's assistant when he moved to the University of Freiburg; it was there that she completed her doctorate degree under his direction. "Husserl had made the old, despised term 'ontology' respectable once more," Herbstrith says,

> just at the hour when the so-called "Christian philosophy" was awakening like Sleeping Beauty from its centuries-old sleep. Through postulating an *a priori* knowledge of essences, he had at one and the same time taken up arms against empiricism, skepticism, and relativism. Enthusiastic young realists had flocked to him, thus creating the "Gottingen School."[254]

Without realizing it, Husserl was creating an intellectual movement that would result in the conversion of many of his students to Christianity.

But it wasn't just Professor Husserl. Edith began attending the lectures of another phenomenologist in Göttingen, Max Scheler (1874–1928), whose views began to exert a stronger influence in philosophical circles than those of Husserl. Scheler, the son of a Lutheran father and a Jewish mother, was filled with admiration for the spiritual beauty of Catholicism, and in his lectures he put religious faith front and center.[255] Religion alone makes the human being human, he said, and humility is the foundation of all moral endeavor. For Edith, this opened up "a whole new realm of 'phenomena' that I wouldn't be able to pass by blindly anymore."[256] She was forced to face her own spiritual poverty, she said later, and she began to wonder if "there actually is a God."[257]

"The bars of the rationalist prejudice I had unconsciously grown up with collapsed," she wrote, "and there, standing in front of me, was the world of faith. I could see that among the inhabitants were people whom I admired, people whom I worked with on a day-to-day basis. That made it worth some serious reflection at the very least."[258]

But letting go of the rationalist blinders took its toll on her. Despite her growing reputation as a phenomenologist in her own right, Edith fell into a state of intense loneliness at this time and suffered bouts of despair. For the first time in her life, she was confronting something she couldn't master by sheer force of will. A feeling of insecurity came over her and she found herself groping in a fog.[259] She wrote later:

> The struggle for clarity went on amid great internal suffering which never gave me a moment's peace day or night. I

even forgot what it meant to get a good night's sleep; it was years before I was able to sleep soundly again. . . . Rational arguments didn't help at all. I couldn't cross the street without hoping to be run over or go hiking without wanting to fall so that I wouldn't have to come back alive.[260]

Then something unexpected happened. Edith was visiting some friends on their farm in Bad Bergzabern, near the French border, and one night she scanned their bookshelves looking for something to read. The book she happened to pull down was *The Autobiography of St. Teresa of Avila*, and she was immediately captivated. She stayed up all night reading and when she finally finished it the next morning, she said to herself: "This is the truth."[261]

What this book did was tell Edith to stop intellectualizing. God does not reveal himself to someone using deductive reasoning, St. Teresa said. He can only be seen by someone who is willing to surrender herself to mystery. The saint explained:

> But before God himself, believe me, a little training in humility . . . means more than all the learning in the world. Instead of establishing proofs and drawing conclusions, we will get to see ourselves honestly for what we are and to remain in simplicity before God. What he wants is for the soul to behave like a fool—which is just what it is in his presence.[262]

Dr. Edith Stein, the well-known phenomenologist, was exhilarated. She immediately bought herself a catechism and Sunday missal and studied them carefully, and then went to her first Mass in the local church in Bad Bergzabern. After Mass, she went to see the pastor, Monsignor Breitling, who quickly recognized that he was talking to an intellectual who would not need much instruction in the faith. On New Year's Day 1922, she was baptized into the Catholic Church—much to the joy of her academic friends and the consternation of her pious Jewish family. Shortly thereafter, she left the world of academia and took a humble job teaching in a training college for girls run by Dominican nuns in Speyer on the River Rhine. She took private vows and began to live like a Dominican among Dominicans, wearing only black and white clothes every day. When she wasn't spending hours in the convent chapel, she was volunteering to help the poor of Speyer in addition to her teaching.

Edith wasn't destined to stay away from the academic world for long, however. A priest friend soon talked her into translating the letters and diaries of Cardinal John Henry Newman from English into German, and then Thomas Aquinas's work *On Truth* from Latin into German. She also resumed her lecturing schedule, speaking in various parts of Germany and Switzerland. Eventually (in 1931) she left the Dominican training college to devote herself full time to academic work and, urged on by friends, applied for a teaching position at the university level. She immediately hit a wall. As a woman in the field of philosophy, she was not taken seriously; some interviewers didn't even bother to read samples of her work. Eventually she accepted a lectureship at the Roman Catholic division of the Institute for Pedagogy at the University of Münster, but before long she hit a wall there also. The Nazis banned all Jews in Germany from holding teaching positions, and that included Jews who had converted to Christianity.

It was at this critical juncture that Edith Stein turned to an idea she had been quietly entertaining for many years, going back to the day of her baptism. She requested entry into the Carmelite convent in Cologne, and was accepted. By then she was forty-two, more than twenty years older than the average Carmelite novice, and far more educated. But she soon

adapted to the strict regimen of the Carmelites, accepting cor-
rection from her superiors with exemplary humility. Over the
next five years, she completed the various steps to final vows as
a Carmelite nun while continuing her writing in philosophy. It
was in that convent that she finished her magnum opus, *Finite
and Eternal Being*, which is a synthesis of the metaphysics of St.
Thomas Aquinas and the phenomenology of Edmund Husserl.

Edith Stein's dream of the contemplative life had finally
come true, but there was one dark cloud that would not leave
her: the unrelenting opposition of her mother. For Auguste Stein,
seeing her daughter become a Catholic was bad enough, but entering a convent added "insult to injury," she said.[263] She could
not understand why her intellectually gifted daughter would
throw her life away in a regressive organization like the Roman
Catholic Church, and she showed her displeasure by refusing to
answer her daughter's weekly letters from the convent. Near the
end of her life, she mellowed slightly by writing an occasional
note at the bottom of letters sent by Rosa, one of Edith's sisters,
but she was still unreconciled when she died on 14 September
1936—the Feast of the Holy Cross for Catholics. Edith, not surprisingly, saw it all as God's mysterious providence. She wrote:

> My mother held to her faith to the very end. The faith and
> firm confidence she had in her God from her earliest child-
> hood until her 87th year remained steadfast, and were the
> last things that stayed alive in her during the final difficult
> agony. Therefore I have the firm belief that she found a
> merciful judge and is now my most faithful helper on my
> way, so that I, too, may reach my goal.[264]

Later that year, Edith was overjoyed by the decision of her
sister Rosa to become a Catholic; Rosa had been postponing
the decision until after her mother's death so as not to add to

her pain. By coincidence, Edith was able to take part in Rosa's instruction in the Catholic faith because she was in hospital at this time with a broken arm and broken leg after falling down a flight of stairs in the convent. In the hospital, the sisters could be together without having to talk through a grille. A few years later, Rosa joined the Carmelites as a Third Order member, and by chance she was living at the same convent complex as Edith when the Nazis came to arrest the two of them in 1942.

Storm Clouds on the Horizon

The Nazi killing machine was ramping up all over Germany, and even nuns living behind the Carmelite grille were not safe. When Adolf Hitler ordered a referendum on his annexation of Austria in 1938, three Nazi officials arrived at Edith's convent in Cologne with voting slips and a list of names. After the vote was taken, the officials counted the slips and asked why Dr. Edith Stein had not voted. The superior naively explained that Edith had a Jewish background, and one of the officials immediately turned to his colleague and said: "Write in here that she is not Aryan."[265] It was an ominous sign. Later that year things got even worse. On November 9, the Night of Broken Glass crashed into the lives of every Jew in Germany and Austria, and Cologne was hit particularly hard. Four synagogues were desecrated and torched in the city that night, dozens of shops were destroyed or looted, and scores of male Jews were arrested without reason or warning.

It was clear to Edith that her presence in the Cologne convent would put the whole community of sisters in danger, and her superior reluctantly looked for a safer place. The Dutch village of Echt, just across the border, turned out to be the best choice, and on New Year's Eve 1938, under the cover of darkness, two friends of the nuns smuggled Edith into Holland by car where she was warmly welcomed at the Echt convent. The sisters in her new community were excited to have a famous philosopher in their midst, and Edith soon found herself giving classes to the novices while continuing her writing. She was deeply grateful to the Echt sisters, she wrote, but she added: "That doesn't mean I'm not constantly aware that we have no lasting dwelling-place" in this world.[266]

Edith Stein had become a fugitive, and she was deeply worried about her future, so much so that she did something people her age don't usually do: she sat down and wrote her last testament. "Already now I joyfully accept the death which God has destined for me in complete submission to his most holy will," she wrote, naming the "Jewish people" and the "salvation of Germany" among the causes for which she wished to die.[267] A decade earlier, at her "clothing ceremony" in Cologne, she had requested "Teresa Benedicta (Blessed) of the Cross" as her religious name, and she chose that name with this precise outcome in mind. Astounding as it may seem, even at that early stage, Edith Stein had a premonition of what her destiny would be. "Of the Cross I saw as referring to the fate of the People of God," she wrote, "which even then was beginning to reveal itself."[268]

A Quiet Sunday in Early August

Sunday, 2 August 1942, looked like any normal Sunday for Edith Stein. She spent the day alternating between periods of praying in the chapel and periods of writing at her desk, as she put some finishing touches on the manuscript *The Science of the Cross*, her book about the life of St. John of the Cross. By late afternoon, she was back in the chapel for prayer, which always began with a reading of some length; it was Edith's turn to take the reading.

That community exercise had barely started when the prioress was called to the parlor, where two SS men asked to see Edith Stein.[269] Assuming that this had to do with some routine emigration forms, the prioress went back to the chapel and interrupted Edith to let her know she was wanted in the parlor. As soon as Edith reached the room, she was ordered (from the other side of the grille) to pack her things immediately and leave with the officers. She and her sister Rosa were under arrest, the two SS men told her, and they had five minutes to get ready.[270] In a state of shock, Edith went back to the chapel, knelt for a moment before the Blessed Sacrament, then turned to the sisters with a red face and calmly said: "Bitte beten, Schwestern!" (Please pray, sisters!).[271]

A couple of the sisters were called from prayer to help Edith pack a few things, while others tried to cook something for her and Rosa. The prioress returned to the parlor and tried to negotiate with the SS, appealing for an extension, but to no avail. "She can either change into something else or come as she is," one of them said. "Give her a blanket, a mug, a spoon and three days' rations."[272] Back in the kitchen, Edith did not feel like eating anything, and Rosa (who by now had been called out of the chapel also) was shaking so much that she wasn't able to eat; one of the nuns fed her scrambled eggs with a spoon. She was as white as a sheet, the nuns said, but Edith continued to be calm. The whole event did not take more than ten or fifteen minutes and, in the confusion, nobody remembered to call the twelve or so nuns who were still in the chapel to say goodbye to the Stein sisters. "Those involved were so dismayed that they did not think of it—everything happened so quickly," one nun said later. "And that is how she was taken from us without saying goodbye. . . . We did not know she was leaving."[273]

Outside, the neighbors had seen the SS men arrive in a military van and they sensed that something bad was happening.

By the time Edith and Rosa were led from the convent, a handful of people had gathered around the gates, incensed at this latest evidence of Nazi brutality, and the first thing they noticed was the fear on Rosa's face. One neighbor recalled hearing Edith say to her sister, "Come, Rosa, we're going for our people," as she held Rosa's hand in a reassuring way.[274] They were immediately taken to the military van parked nearby, and when the Steins got in, they saw two nuns already locked inside. A fleet of vans had been crisscrossing the country that Sunday arresting Catholic Jews in retaliation for a pastoral letter issued by the Dutch bishops protesting the anti-Jewish policies of the Nazis.[275]

From the convent in Echt, the four women, all dressed in religious habits, were driven directly to police headquarters in Roermond where they were joined by other Catholic Jews (religious and lay) who had been arrested in Maastricht that day. From there, the prisoners were taken in two vans to Amersfoort concentration camp, a transit facility in a remote area. The drivers got lost and did not get there until 3 a.m., while the terrified prisoners spent hours in dark vans, not knowing where they were going or what their fate would be.

Next Stop Westerbork

The prisoners didn't stay very long at Amersfoort. On the afternoon of that same day, they were packed onto a passenger train with some eleven hundred other prisoners, still clueless about where they were going. Because the curtains were kept closed, they could not read the names of the stations they were passing; rumors abounded about their destination being in some part of Germany. Eventually they stopped near a train station, and were ordered to walk for about an hour to a camp in the middle of nowhere. They had arrived at Westerbork, a transit camp in northeastern Netherlands, but none of them had ever heard of the place. It was impossible by now to know exactly how many Catholic Jews were in this large group of prisoners, but those in religious habits stood out: two priests, two brothers, eight nuns, and two Third Order members. All of them had a yellow six-pointed Star of David attached to their habits.

The camp registration procedure began immediately, taking the prisoners "from table to table, filling out all kinds of useless forms."[276] After being photographed while holding up a prison identification number (Edith's was 44074), the prisoners were herded into crude drafty barracks that were as filthy as the ones they had left in Amersfoort, with iron bunks stacked in triple decks.

One of the biggest sources of stress was the separation of husbands and wives, which caused unrestrained weeping among the women. But they found some consolation in the presence of the priests and nuns who continued to pray as a group and showed kindness to their fellow prisoners. "Edith Stein went among the women like an angel, comforting, helping, and consoling them," one survivor said later. "Many of the mothers were on the brink of insanity and had sat moaning for days, without giving any thought to their children. Edith Stein immediately set about taking care of these little ones. She washed them, combed their hair, and tried to make sure they were fed and cared for."[277] She was, in short, like another Etty Hillesum for the inmates of Westerbork.

Meanwhile Etty herself, who was working in Westerbork at this time, was fascinated by the unexpected appearance of the priests and nuns wearing the yellow star on their habits. "I remember two young novices, twins, with identical beautiful, dark ghetto faces and serene, childish eyes peering out from under their skullcaps," she wrote. "They said with mild surprise that they had been fetched at half past four from morning mass, and that they had eaten red cabbage in Amersfoort."[278]

> There was a priest, still fairly young, who had not left his monastery for fifteen years.[279] He was out in the "world" for the first time, and I stood next to him for a while, following his eyes as they wandered peacefully around the barracks where the newcomers were being received. . . . "And what do you think of the world now?" I asked. But his gaze remained unwavering and friendly above the brown habit, as if everything he saw was known, familiar from long ago.[280]

That same evening, some of the priests were seen walking "one behind the other in the dusk between the dark barracks. . . . They were saying their rosaries as imperturbably as if they had just finished vespers at the monastery," Etty wrote. "And isn't it true that one can pray anywhere, in a wooden barracks just as well as in a stone monastery, or indeed, anywhere on this earth, where God, in these troubled times, feels like casting his likeness."[281]

En Route to Auschwitz

Edith Stein and her fellow converts were soon herded onto a freight train for the torturous three-day journey to Auschwitz in Poland. It was Friday morning, 7 August 1942.[282] As usual, seventy or eighty people were packed into each car so that people could scarcely breathe, and the only light that entered the carriages was what filtered in between the narrow wooden slats, or a small opening up high. Prisoners begged for a drink of water whenever the train stopped at a station, but onlookers who wanted to help were kept at a distance by the Nazi guards.

An eyewitness account of Edith's train surfaced during the commemoration of the fortieth anniversary of her death in 1982, and it merits quoting here. On that occasion, a soldier by the name of Johannes Wieners came forward to claim that he remembered speaking to Edith Stein while passing through the station in Breslau on 7 August 1942. While his train was stopped for refueling, another train pulled in alongside it; when the guard opened one of the sliding doors, he saw a large group of prisoners, penned up and listlessly squatting on the floor. Here is Wieners' description of what happened next:

> There was a horrible stench coming from the car. A woman dressed like a nun appeared at the door, and, I guess because I looked sympathetic to her, she said to me: "It's terrible. We don't even have containers to relieve ourselves." After that, she looked into the distance at Breslau and said: "This is my home town; I'll never see it again." I stared at her, wondering what she was talking about. She paused for a minute, then said: "We are going to our death." That really shook me. I remember that I asked her: "Do the other prisoners know about this?" She answered very slowly: "It's better for them not to know."[283]

The Killing Center

After three days, the train finally arrived at the platform of the Birkenau facility, situated a short distance from the original camp in Auschwitz.[284] It was Sunday, 9 August, and the Steins and their companions had not had a shower or change of clothes for an entire week. The only food they had had was what they were able to grab when they were arrested without warning. They were sleep-deprived and seriously dehydrated. Neither had they had Mass or Communion, not since the previous Sunday when the SS arrived at the convent gate without warning. Since then, their prayers had been sporadic and distracted. In the camps they had been able to pray together in groups, but on the train all they could do was close their eyes and put themselves in the hands of God. It had been a week filled with unspeakable horror: the crude language and cruelty of the SS guards at every turn; the torture of not being able to sit down properly, let alone sleep, in the freight car; the stench that built up in the car over three days of travel without toilet facilities. And now, as the guards kicked them off the train with yells and rifle butts, there was the smell of burning flesh everywhere.

The gas chambers at this time were situated in the corner of an orchard in Birkenau, about two miles from the original Auschwitz camp, deliberately placed so that the prisoners in Auschwitz could not hear the screams of the victims being gassed. The Nazis had renovated two old cottages, walling up the doors and windows and gutting the insides to create sealed spaces that could be used as chambers for mass extermination. New entrances were created with heavy airtight doors, and hatches were opened high up on the walls to allow crystals of Zyklon B to be thrown in by guards wearing gas masks. Zyklon B, a cyanide compound that was used to kill rats and cockroaches, proved to be a cheap and efficient way of killing humans also. As soon as the Zyklon pellets were exposed to the air, they released a gas that killed people in ten or fifteen minutes.

These two gas chambers, known as the "Little Red House" and the "Little White House," began operation in mid-March of 1942 and, small as they were, the Nazis could cram in hundreds of victims at a time, 800 in one house and 1200 in the other. Both had ventilation systems to clear out the residual gas promptly, after which the workers entered to remove the dead bodies and wash the vomit and excrement off the walls and floor. This step was important because the Nazis wanted the chambers to look like shower facilities, complete with fake pipes overhead. They used this trick to control the crowds. Rather than pushing a large number of screaming people into a gas chamber by force, it was easier to give them a friendly talk explaining that, after their arduous train journey, they would now be able to take a nice hot shower. One Holocaust survivor, Thomas "Toivi" Blatt, described how a sweet-talking SS officer in Sobibor concentration camp was able to calm the nerves of three thousand Jews who had just been pushed off a cattle train from the Netherlands:

> Then they went straight to a big yard and there a German we call "the angel of death" talked to them so nicely. He apologized for the three-day journey from Holland but now he said they're in a beautiful place, because Sobibor is always beautiful. And then he said "For sanitary reasons you need to have a shower, and later you will get orders to leave here." Then people clapped, "Bravo," and they undressed themselves nicely. . . . They didn't know that they will die in a few minutes. Then they were told to go on from the barracks just a few [steps] to the gas chamber. This trap was so perfect that I'm sure that when they were in the gas chamber and gas came out instead of water, probably they were thinking that this was some kind of malfunction.[285]

Blatt and the other Jewish prisoners who were forced to work in the gas chambers and crematoria under threat of death were called Sonderkommandos." There were about 250 of them working in the Little Red House and the Little White House when Edith and Rosa Stein were taken there. (That number increased to 900 when the four larger gas chamber facilities were opened.) Part of their job was to reassure the new arrivals as they lined up for the "shower," and then bury the bodies in shallow pits nearby—something that turned out to be a serious problem. When the summer heat came, those shallow graves became a source of pollution in the Birkenau neighborhood, much to the embarrassment of Commandant Rudolf Höss and his crew. They needed to find a solution fast, before the world found out about their crimes, so they decided to burn the bodies in newly created pits. The Sonderkommandos never received any perks for doing this horrifying work, said Otto Pressburger, another Sonderkommando, but apparently the Nazi guards did. "The SS men were constantly drinking vodka or cognac or something else from bottles," he said. "They could not cope with it, either."[286]

The Little Red House and the Little White House were eventually replaced by a much larger purpose-built facility that raised the extermination program to an industrial level. The two renovated cottages were only in operation for about a year, from spring of 1942 to spring of 1943, but it was in the middle of that year (9 August 1942) that Edith and Rosa Stein were taken to Auschwitz-Birkenau. It is a fair assumption, then, that they were killed in one of these cottages.

The Death of a Martyr

Based on the memories of Auschwitz survivors such as those quoted above, we have a fairly clear idea of how Edith Stein— Sr. Teresa Benedicta of the Cross—and her sister Rosa were killed. They were kicked off the train, taken to the two renovated cottages in the orchard, and given the usual promise of a hot shower before bed. It is doubtful that Edith was fooled by such a promise, however, given her knowledge of the Nazi state and the smell of burning flesh everywhere. The prisoners were then sent to a makeshift dressing room or designated outdoor area, and directed to enter the "shower room" (one of the two renovated cottages). When prisoners were packed tightly in the chamber, a Sonderkommando locked the heavy airtight door from the outside.

When the Zyklon B pellets were thrown in through the hatch high up on the wall, many prisoners began to scream as they realized that it was not a shower facility after all. According to *The Holocaust Encyclopedia*, the cyanide interfered with the ability of cells to absorb oxygen, which meant that the victims automatically breathed faster in an effort to take in more oxygen. Because their bodies were instead taking in more and more of the cyanide-laden air, the victims eventually went silent and lost consciousness. Seizures and cardiac arrest finally killed them, with those nearest the wall (where the hatches were) dying first.[287]

Thus were Edith and her sister Rosa numbered among the thousands of anonymous victims of the Auschwitz-Birkenau killing center, leaving no grave by which friends and family could remember them. Edith was fifty years old and Rosa fifty-eight. A laconic communiqué announcing Edith's death said this: "Auschwitz, number 44074. August 9, 1942, in Poland, Stein died, Edith Therese Hedwig, born October 12, 1891 at Breslau, resident at Echt."[288] (She had adopted the name of her friend, Therese Hedwig, on the day of her Baptism.)

But as God's providence would have it, Edith Stein was not an anonymous number for long. Twenty years later her canonization process was initiated by Cardinal Josef Frings of Cologne, and in 1998 Pope John Paul II canonized her as a martyr in St. Peter's Basilica in Rome. In October 2006, his successor, Pope Benedict XVI, dedicated a monument to her memory that is mightier than any gravestone. It is a large marble statue that fills one of the last vacant exterior niches in the western facade of

St. Peter's Basilica, next to the statue of St. Teresa of Ávila. The statue is a combination of Jewish and Christian symbols: Edith is holding both a Torah scroll with the words *Shema Yisrael* ("Hear, O Israel")[289] and a cross topped by a crown of thorns.

Two Intellectuals with Much in Common

Etty Hillesum and Edith Stein were two very different personalities. Etty was a free spirit, with no formal religious background, who had a passionate love affair with another free spirit double her age. Edith, on the other hand, had an iron will and tireless self-control and seems never to have had an inappropriate sexual thought in her life. Etty wrote a free-flowing diary and some letters that lay hidden in an attic for forty years, while Edith wrote numerous books on philosophy and the lives of the saints (enough to fill about two dozen volumes in German), and became a famous philosopher in her own lifetime. These two intellectuals, from neighboring countries and twenty years apart in age, had very different backgrounds and very different histories. Nevertheless, their tireless searches for God have significant parallels. Here are some of them:

Both concluded that thinking alone was not enough. Etty's experience under the chestnut tree, described in chapter 3, convinced her that in her struggle to find meaning in life she needed to stop intellectualizing and "just let it happen to me."[290] You shouldn't live on your brains alone, she concluded, but "on deeper, more abiding sources."[291] Edith used similar language describing how she struggled with the existence of God. After overworking her powerful intellect for years and getting nowhere, she finally discovered "a state of resting in God, an absolute break with all intellectual activity, when one forms no plans, makes no decisions and for the first time really ceases to act."[292] They both discovered that you can't just think yourself into heaven.

Both found meaning in suffering and death. Etty didn't use the language of a theologian, but she saw suffering as redemptive. She was determined not to waste her energies on "the fear of death or the refusal to accept its inevitability." It sounds paradoxical, she wrote (as we saw in chapter 4), but "by excluding death from our life we cannot live a full life, and by admitting death into our life we enlarge and enrich it."[293] Edith's last testimony says the same thing but in precise theological terms: "Everyone has to suffer and die. And if he is a living member of the Body of Christ, then his death and suffering acquire redemptive power through the divine nature of the Head. In the light of the mystery of redemption, [this] is the ultimate raison d'etre."[294]

Both practiced detachment in preparation for being sent to a concentration camp. Etty's diary has many reflections on the luxuries she would have to give up if she were sent to a concentration camp. "More and more we must learn to do without those of our physical necessities that are not absolutely vital," she wrote.[295] Edith was more reticent about her preparations, but early risers in the Echt convent remember seeing a nun kneeling in prayer with her arms outstretched. It was an open secret that Edith had for a long time been quietly training herself for life in a concentration camp by enduring cold and hunger.[296]

Both were mystics who found God within themselves. Etty and Edith both used the image of an inner space. "There is a really deep well inside me and in it dwells God," Etty wrote, as we saw in chapter 3. "Sometimes I am there, too. But more often stones and grit block the well, and God is buried beneath. Then he must be dug out."[297] Edith also described a God who was within but hidden. Anyone who wishes to find God, she said, "will withdraw into the barren solitude of the inner self, to dwell in the darkness of faith through a simple loving glance of the spirit at God, who is present although concealed."[298]

Both radiated an unusual interior peace. "You always look so radiant," an inmate in Westerbork said to Etty one day.[299] "You have made me so rich, Oh God," she wrote, "please let me share out Your beauty with open hands."[300] Edith developed the same reputation, even in the four short days she spent in Westerbork. She stood out because of her "complete calm and self-possession."[301] One observer said, "The glow of a saintly Carmelite radiated from her eyes."[302]

Both said that love must conquer all. "Each of us must turn inward and destroy in himself all that he thinks he ought to destroy in others," Etty wrote. "And remember that every atom of hate we add to this world makes it still more inhospitable."[303] Edith said the same thing in much the same words. "Hatred must never be given the last word," she often said. Somehow it had to be possible, she observed, to obtain through prayer and atonement the grace of conversion for those who hated.[304]

Both gave their lives for their people. When Etty's old friend Klaas Smelik physically grabbed her one day and tried to convince her not to go to Westerbork, she made her intentions very clear. "You don't understand me," she said. "I want to share the destiny of my people."[305] Edith's last testament had the same determination: "I joyfully accept in advance the death God has appointed for me . . . for the Jewish people."[306] And when the Nazis unexpectedly arrived at the convent in Echt to arrest her, as we saw, she calmly said to her sister: "Come, Rosa, we're going for our people."[307]

Chapter 6

Life in Auschwitz-Birkenau: Three Months of Starvation and Abuse

In the last chapter we listed the many ways in which the life stories of Etty Hillesum and Edith Stein were similar, reflecting a common path to God and a commitment to give their lives for their people. But there was one important difference between the two. By the time Edith Stein was taken to Auschwitz-Birkenau extermination camp, her pilgrimage in this world had come to an end. She and her sister were killed in the gas chambers as soon as they arrived. Etty Hillesum faced a different fate. She arrived a year later, when Germany's war economy had a greater need for forced labor, and she was one of those singled out as an able-bodied worker. That meant that she spent close to three months in slave labor camps in the Auschwitz-Birkenau industrial complex, and presumably died a slow death from starvation and physical abuse.

We will never know what exact work she did, nor the exact circumstances of her death. Even the date of her death is a rough estimate by the Red Cross. But we do know a lot about Auschwitz-Birkenau from the stories of victims who survived it and the research of historians since World War II. From that information we can describe in considerable detail what life was like there in 1943. It was very different from what Etty knew in Westerbork.

By 1943, the Birkenau facility, which was about two miles from the original Auschwitz camp, had seen some significant changes, the most important of which was the huge purpose-built gas chamber and crematorium complex in which staggering numbers of victims could be murdered in one day. Dozens of new barracks were also constructed, making Birkenau (also known as Auschwitz II), a much larger camp than the original one. When exhausted prisoners arrived at Birkenau, the first things they saw were giant chimneys that belched flames into the sky. And if the smell from those chimneys didn't unnerve the new arrivals, the reception they got from the officials on the platform certainly did.

"Abruptly, the door opened," Elie Wiesel began his account of the arrival of his train:

> Strange-looking creatures, dressed in striped jackets and black pants, jumped into the wagon. Holding flashlights and sticks, they began to strike at us left and right, shouting: "Everybody out! Leave everything inside. Hurry up!" We jumped out. . . . In front of us, those flames. In the air, the smell of burning flesh. It must have been around midnight. We had arrived. In Birkenau.[308]

The prisoners were immediately ordered to form two lines, one for men and the other for women and children. At the top of those long lines were SS officers whose job it was to divide the prisoners into two new lines that went in opposite directions. One of the new lines led directly to the gas chambers while the other line was for those who would be put in slave labor units. In other words, one line was for the living and the other for the dead, and each prisoner's fate was decided in a matter of seconds. An SS guard gave a nod of the head or a gesture with his finger to go in one direction or the other. All elderly prisoners and most children were automatically directed into the line for the dead. In fact, the majority of prisoners were sent to that line, all except the most able-bodied men and women and some children who would be used for medical experiments. The children were immediately taken away by the notorious Dr. Josef Mengele or his colleagues, while those singled out for work were directed to a special barracks, known as "quarantine," to await further processing.

The newly arrived prisoners had no idea what these lines meant, of course. Exhausted after several days in crowded cattle cars, they had just two things on their minds: Would they get their bits of luggage back, and would families be allowed to stay together?

"Tearing apart families, separating the men from the women and children, caused great unrest and excitement in the entire transport," Commandant Höss wrote in his memoir.

> Separating those who were able to work only increased the seriousness of the situation. No matter what, the families wanted to stay together. So it happened that even those selected to work ran back to the other members of their family, or the mothers with their children tried to get back to their husbands, or to the older children. Often there was such chaos and confusion that the selection process had to be started all over again.[309]

If necessary, order was restored by brute force, Höss wrote, as victims gradually realized the awful truth about their destiny.

Etty Hillesum presumably was sent to the quarantine barracks, where she had to hand over any valuables she might have had, such as a wristwatch and jewelry, and she was ordered to take off all her clothes. All the hair on her body was shaved, and she was given a striped pajama-style uniform to put on. Then she was registered as a prisoner, and her identification number was tattooed on her left arm. Auschwitz was the only camp to adopt this tattoo method rather than using a disk around the neck, probably because of the high mortality rate among the forced labor victims. It was more efficient to identify a corpse from a tattoo than to depend on a disk that could become detached and get lost.[310]

But worrisome as this process was, Etty was probably more concerned about her family than herself. What happened to her parents and her brother? Which line were they put in? On the train, the Hillesum family had been separated, which was what Etty had wanted because she did not want to see her parents suffer. For that reason, she had boarded wagon 12 while her parents and brother were in wagon 1. Historians believe that, because of their ages, her parents either died during the grueling three-day journey or were gassed as soon as they arrived in Birkenau. Presumably Mischa was chosen for slave labor, because he did not die until March 1944, several months after Etty. How much contact Etty had with her brother, if any, we will never know. Auschwitz-Birkenau was a large complex, and the men and women were kept in separate barracks (there were up to 30,000 female prisoners there at any one time).

The Auschwitz-Birkenau Industrial Complex

The Nazis were focusing on able-bodied workers at this time for a reason. By 1943, with the disastrous defeat of the Germans in the Battle of Stalingrad and the growing realization that they might not win the war after all, Germany needed more workers for its war efforts. The SS in particular needed workers because of its industrial and agricultural enterprises operating in the Auschwitz area. Slave labor was a welcome gift for digging ditches, draining ponds, and shoring up riverbanks (the area was prone to flooding). In addition, IG Farben, the German chemical and pharmaceutical conglomerate, was operating a factory nearby for synthetic rubber (needed for the war), and its executives had had slave labor in mind when they chose Birkenau for its location. Other industries followed IG Farben, forming a network of some three dozen satellite camps around the main one, all with the same interest in slave labor as they planned massive expansion programs.

A business arrangement was set up whereby Auschwitz inmates were allocated to these factories by the Nazis for a fixed price, payable to the SS. By this time, the camp population had grown from 25,000 to 85,000, about half of whom were Jewish and the rest a mixture of Soviet POWs, Polish dissidents, Roma, and other targeted groups such as the physically disabled, Catholic priests, and the intelligentsia.[311] Because the working conditions were so horrific, the turnover in the labor force was high, with a life expectancy of only a couple of months. These forced labor units were in effect an extermination program by another name, mass killing that took several months rather than several minutes.

Life in the slave labor force was a mixture of dehumanization and terror. Colored patches were used to distinguish the various types of prisoners: red for political opponents, violet for Jehovah's Witnesses, green for criminals, black for "asocials" (including vagrants and Roma), pink for homosexual people, yellow for Jews. The Jews were looked on as subhuman by everyone, guards and prisoners alike, and they were subjected to a level of ill treatment that non-Jews were not.[312] Everyone, Jew or not, was known by an assigned number, and every hour of the day was controlled by a cadre of supervisors called Kapos. These Kapos were Jewish prisoners who had been carefully chosen for the position by the Nazis because of their toughness and cruelty. In reality the Kapos did the dirty work for the Nazi guards, and they were often more brutal than the Nazis themselves. As Heinrich Himmler, the architect of the concentration camp system, put it: "His [the Kapo's] job is to see that the work gets done . . . thus he has to push his men. As soon as we are no longer satisfied with him, he is no longer a Kapo and returns to the other inmates. He knows that they will beat him to death his first night back."[313]

Otto Pressburger, a young Czechoslovakian prisoner who was quoted in the last chapter, witnessed an incident of Kapo brutality that was seared into his memory his first day in the camp. His unit, which was building roads, included a young Jew from a wealthy family who had gold teeth. As soon as the Kapo spotted the teeth, he said he wanted that gold. The prisoner said several times that that was not possible, and eventually the Kapo became furious. He took a shovel and hit the prisoner over the head several times until he fell down. Then he put the shovel on his throat and stood on it, and after breaking his neck he used the shovel to pry the teeth out of his mouth. When another Jew standing nearby asked him how he could do such a thing, the Kapo said he would show him. He walked over and killed that prisoner in the same way. Then he told the rest of the unit never to ask questions. "That evening we had to carry twelve bodies with us back to the barracks," Pressburger said. "He killed them just for fun. All this happened the first day at work."[314]

The Daily Routine

Work days began about two hours before dawn with roll call, and could be eleven hours long, with just a half hour for lunch. The food consisted of a meager ration of bread, a coffee substitute, and a watery soup made with cabbage, turnips, carrots, and potato peels, three times a day if they were lucky; sometimes it was only two meals, or just one.[315] The soup was frequently inedible, and there was never enough of it. It was a woefully inadequate diet for workers doing heavy manual labor while exposed to bitter cold in inadequate clothing.

Hunger was a constant reality, so much so that when the guards were not watching and workers had a chance to talk, they often talked about food. "One fellow would ask another working next to him in the ditch what his favorite recipes were," Viktor Frankl wrote later. "Then they would exchange recipes and plan the menu for the day when they would have a reunion—the day in the distant future when they would be liberated and returned home."[316] Some resorted to cannibalism. Commandant Höss remembered coming across the body of a Soviet POW that had been torn open with a dull instrument. "The liver was missing," he wrote matter-of-factly. "They beat each other to death just to get something to eat."[317] Thirst was also a constant affliction. Some survivors described the double pain of wanting to drink the water on the ground, but knowing that it was lethal because it was so foul.[318]

Not surprisingly, prisoners exposed to these conditions soon began to look like skeletons dressed in rags, as "the last layers of subcutaneous fat had vanished," and their bodies began to devour themselves. "The organism digested its own protein, and the muscles disappeared," Frankl explained. "Then the body had no powers of resistance left. One after another the members of the little community in our hut died. Each of us could calculate with fair accuracy whose turn would be next, and when his own would come."[319] If death didn't come from overwork and malnutrition, it came from arbitrary beatings. A prisoner could be beaten to death just because an SS guard or Kapo didn't like the way she looked at him. And from the Nazi viewpoint, this high mortality rate was just fine. Prisoners were expendable, they said, and could easily be replaced. Pavel Stenkin, a Soviet

POW who survived, remembered this presence of death more than anything: "When it was time to get up in the morning, those who were alive moved, and around them would be two or three dead people. You go to bed and you are alive, and by the morning you are dead. It was death, death, death. Death at night, death in the morning, death in the afternoon. There was death all the time."[320]

Block 11 represented the most terrifying way to die. It was the punishment barracks, to which prisoners were sent for any kind of infraction, even something as minor as taking an extra piece of bread off the ground. The Nazi in charge of the block, Maximilian Grabner, was one of the most notorious sadists in the camp, and when it came to torture he had a variety of methods in his tool kit: whipping, water torture, putting needles under their fingernails, pouring petrol over them and setting them alight. A favorite method of his was holding a prisoner's head on a hot stove as a way of extracting information. Seeing the results of these tortures had an enormous effect on other prisoners, who were terrified to even walk past Block 11. (When Pope John Paul II visited Auschwitz-Birkenau in 1979, Block 11 was his particular focus. He stopped to pray in the basement cell where St. Maximilian Kolbe was tortured and murdered in 1941.)

The work day ended as it began, with roll call conducted out in the open, regardless of the weather. Prisoners were called out by number and if an individual could not be accounted for, the process went on for as long as it took to find an explanation. Exhausted prisoners might stand for long periods in the snow on a winter night because a prisoner was missing. The prisoners' only respite was sleep, when they finally got that far, but the sleeping conditions were as disgusting as everything else in the camp: "rough wooden bunks, sometimes with a bit of rancid, lice-infested straw, or a threadbare soiled blanket."[321] Each bunk was crowded three or four deep. And what did a prisoner dream about? "Of bread, cake, cigarettes, and nice warm baths," says Viktor Frankl. "The lack of having these simple desires satisfied led him to seek wish-fulfillment in dreams."[322]

For one Hungarian survivor, Alice Lok Cahana, the desire for a warm bath was as urgent as the desire for food. Her reason was the atrocious hygiene. "By then we were infested with lice, and it felt so horrible—horrible," she said. "Nothing can be so humiliating as when you feel your whole body is infested. Your head, your clothes—everywhere you look on your body there's an animal crawling. And you cannot wash it off. There's no water."[323] What passed for bathrooms were disgusting cement holes or ditches. Since dysentery was epidemic, prisoners were in constant need of latrines and rarely reached them in time because visits were timed and limited.[324]

This was the world Etty Hillesum found herself in during the fall of 1943. For a year prior, she had thought about what might be in store for her in a camp like this, and she had tried to prepare herself for it. She had practiced small acts of detachment, giving up her scented soap, her favorite blouse, her lipstick, in order to be ready for a spartan life. But was she ready for this? Could any human being be fully ready for Auschwitz-Birkenau in 1943?

The inmates who survived this savagery could only do so by having a steely determination to live through one more day, no matter what it took. They had to have strong minds. Many prisoners could not muster up that kind of determination and committed suicide by throwing themselves against the electric fence on the perimeter. Certain kinds of work increased a prisoner's chances of survival, of course, but getting them required a mountain of good luck. Any kind of indoor job, away from the bitter cold, was desirable. And if one happened to get a job in "Canada," one was doubly fortunate, insofar as that can be said of a prisoner.

"Canada" was the place where the confiscated luggage of the newly arrived prisoners was gathered. (It was so called because that country was considered a dreamland of unimaginable riches.) In that department, the suitcases and rucksacks were searched for money and valuables that might have been hidden in the lining of clothes or sewn into false pockets, and those valuables were shipped to Berlin for use by the Nazi state. The inmates who were chosen to work there did not have to wear the prison uniform and were allowed to keep their hair unshaved. "Actually, working in 'Canada' saved my life because we had food, we got water and we could take a shower there," said Linda Breder from Czechoslovakia, who was nineteen years old when she began working in "Canada." After spending the previous year working outdoors, her new job was a gift—even interesting at times:

> Every piece had to be searched—underwear, everything. And we found lots of diamonds, gold, coins, dollars— foreign currency from all over Europe. And when we found something we had to put it in a wooden box with a slit that was in the middle of the barracks. . . . Nobody else was aware of all the wealth and clothes arriving. Only us. Some 600 girls who used to work there.[325]

Not all of the confiscated valuables went to Berlin, however. Corruption was widespread in "Canada," both among the SS and among the inmates. The SS took many an armful of goods home to their wives and children: money, jewelry, expensive clothes, food. Little wonder Commandant Höss's wife called Auschwitz "Paradise," and stayed on in the villa when her husband was transferred to Berlin.[326] The girls working in "Canada" also smuggled out some of the clothes to give to their friends who had to work outdoors; sturdy shoes and warm underwear were desired most. But the most important perk was the food they found: canned goods, chocolates, liquor. "Yes, we ate that food," Breder said with some guilt:

> It was a rescue for us. . . . We wanted to live. We wanted to survive. Should we have thrown it away? We didn't kill anyone. We ate only their food. They were already dead at this time. . . . To have food, water and enough sleep—those were the things we cared about. We had all that in "Canada."327

This is where Etty's knapsack ended up, but the prisoners probably didn't find much that they would consider valuable. The books they found were probably thrown away, as Etty faced a life with nothing to read and no notebooks to write in. For Etty it was unthinkable. And yet she had already considered it, more than a year before. "The worst thing for me will be when I am no longer allowed pencil and paper to clarify my thoughts," she wrote in July 1942. "They are absolutely indispensable to me, for without them I shall fall apart and be utterly destroyed. But now I know that once you begin to lower your demands and your expectations, you can let go of everything."328 Even if Etty had been allowed to have books and notebooks, there was little opportunity to enjoy them, given the long hours of labor on top of long periods of twice-daily roll calls.

There were some other jobs, besides "Canada," that inmates considered desirable. A job in the kitchen granted access to extra food. The women and girls in the brothel also had better food, but it came with the soul-destroying cost of forced prostitution. The idea for brothels in some of the camps had come from SS leader Heinrich Himmler, who wanted to increase productivity by offering hard-working prisoners an incentive to work even harder.[329] Jews were barred from having any part in this Himmler plan, either as prostitutes or as "customers."

How Some Prisoners Found Meaning

Man's Search for Meaning by Viktor Frankl is one of the most influential books ever published on the Holocaust. More than fifteen million copies have been printed in some twenty-four languages since it was first published in German in 1946. I read the early English edition when I was in college over fifty years ago, and I reread it recently while writing this book.

In the book, Frankl, a Holocaust survivor who spent time in four different camps including Auschwitz and Dachau, develops an important insight about human survival. Forces beyond your control, such as the Nazis, can strip you of everything except for one thing, he says. They cannot take away your freedom to choose how you respond to their cruelty. They can do indescribable damage to you on the outside, but they cannot damage you on the inside, unless you let them. To put it another way, the prisoners best equipped to handle the brutality of concentration camps were not those who were physically robust but those who were spiritually strong, those who could rely on an inner life of spiritual freedom.

This was not easy to do, Frankl admits. In a system which did not value human life and which reduced prisoners to objects for extermination, many prisoners began to lose their moral values and sense of human dignity. They focused on one thing only: survival for themselves and their friends. Everything else was sacrificed to that one goal. "If the man in the concentration camp did not struggle against this in a last effort to save his self-respect, he lost the feeling of being an individual, a being with a mind, with inner freedom and personal value," Frankl writes. "He thought of himself then as only part of an enormous mass of people; his existence descended to the level of animal life."[330] Every day, every hour, offered the opportunity to make a decision about whether or not a prisoner would submit to those powers that tried to rob him of his very self and make him nothing more than a plaything of circumstances.[331]

Frankl uses his own experience to illustrate the point. One morning after roll call and a bowl of watery soup, the workers in his unit were summoned with the usual nerve-wracking shout: "Detachment, forward march! Left-two-three-four! Left-two-three-four!" He and his unit immediately began the daily march to a building site (which could be miles away), stumbling in the darkness over stones on the frozen mud surface. The guards kept shouting at them and driving them faster with their rifle butts, and anyone with sore feet had to find support on the arm of a neighbor. That particular morning, the man marching next to Frankl whispered to him: "If our wives could see us now! I do hope they are better off in their camps and don't know what is happening to us."[332] That comment led Frankl to think of his own wife. Nothing more was said between the men, but each knew that the other was thinking about home. Frankl continues:

> Occasionally, I looked at the sky, where the stars were fading and the pink light of the morning was beginning to spread behind a dark bank of clouds. But my mind clung to my wife's image, imagining it with uncanny acuteness. I heard her answering me, saw her smile, her frank and encouraging look. Real or not, her look was then more luminous than the sun which was beginning to rise.[333]

The experience was enough to move him to tears, he writes, as a new realization dawned on him, an epiphany that transformed the desolation and spiritual poverty around him. For the first time in his life, he saw the truth

> as it is set into song by so many poets, proclaimed as the final wisdom by so many thinkers. The truth—that love is the ultimate and the highest goal to which man can aspire. Then I grasped the meaning of the greatest secret that human poetry and human thought and belief can impart: *The salvation of man is through love and in love.*

Frankl began to understand how a man who has nothing left in this world still may know bliss, be it only for a brief moment, by contemplating the image of someone he truly loves.[334]

Along with this realization came an unusual sensitivity to the beauty of creation. One day when he and other prisoners were being taken to a new camp in Bavaria, their train brought them past the mountains of Salzburg "with their summits glowing in the sunset." The prisoners happened to glance out the barred windows of the prison car and were awed by the beauty before them. If someone had seen their faces at that moment, Frankl writes, "he would never have believed that those were the faces of men who had given up all hope of life and liberty. Despite that factor—or maybe because of it—we were carried away by nature's beauty, which we had missed for so long."[335]

Frankl goes on to quote a famous Jewish philosopher. When he thinks of the prisoners who never lost hope, he says, he remembers something Baruch Spinoza once said: that "suffering ceases to be suffering as soon as we form a clear and precise picture of it."[336] The prisoners Frankl admired most were those who did just that. They were people who could rise above their suffering, look at it objectively, as from a distance, and thus give it a purpose. This heroic inner achievement, Frankl writes, was a testament to the fact that a meaningful life could be found even in a Nazi concentration camp. Here are Frankl's very significant words: "If there is a meaning in life at all, then there must be a meaning in suffering. Suffering is an ineradicable part of life, even as fate and death. Without suffering and death human life cannot be complete."[337]

Where have we heard that language before? Remember what Etty Hillesum said about those who try to run away from suffering and death:

> Through non-acceptance and through having all those fears, most people are left with just a pitiful and mutilated slice of life, which can hardly be called life at all. It sounds paradoxical: by excluding death from our life we cannot live a full life, and by admitting death into our life we enlarge and enrich it.[338]

Etty Hillesum and Viktor Frankl both saw suffering as redemptive. In Etty's case, that insight was more premeditated. Before she ever got to a concentration camp, she had spent a year or more preparing herself for such a place. "I am ready for everything, for anywhere on this earth, wherever God may send me," she had written in July 1942, as she perfected the art of withdrawal into her inner dwelling.[339] And four days later she wrote:

> I shall always feel safe in God's arms. They may well succeed in breaking me physically, but no more than that. I may face cruelty and deprivation the likes of which I cannot imagine in even my wildest fantasies. Yet all this is as nothing to the immeasurable expanse of my faith in God and my inner receptiveness. I shall always be able to stand on my own two feet even when they are planted on the hardest soil of the harshest reality.[340]

Etty's feet were indeed planted on the hardest soil of the harshest reality. We know now that the particular transport that took her to Auschwitz (on 7 September 1943) had a worse survival rate than most of the transports, especially for women. Of the 987 victims (including 170 children) who were taken on that train, only eight survived Auschwitz-Birkenau: "The women who were put to work were given such heavy tasks that their 'life expectancy' was estimated at a maximum of two months."[341] For Etty it was a bit longer; she survived almost three months. We can only imagine what her physical appearance was like by then, as the young woman who had charmed so many people with her beauty, and inspired them with her dynamic personality, was reduced to a pitiful skeleton with a gaunt face by the horrible conditions and hard labor imposed by the Nazis of Auschwitz-Birkenau. We will never have a precise answer as to the manner of her death, but we can say with confidence that she had prepared herself for that place of horror, and her studies and contemplation ensured that she understood the meaning of suffering and was ready to embrace it.

"It doesn't matter whether my untrained body will be able to carry on, that is really of secondary importance," she wrote in July 1942. "The main thing is that even if we die a terrible death we are able to feel right up to the very last moment that life has meaning and beauty, that we have realized our potential and lived a good life."[342]

Epilogue

What Happened to the Pivotal Players?

Following is a brief account of what happened to the other people in our story after the war.

Mischa Hillesum, Etty's youngest brother, was brought to Auschwitz-Birkenau on the same train as Etty and their parents. He died on 31 March 1944. Presumably, like Etty, he was the victim of starvation, exhaustion, and physical abuse. Etty's *brother Jaap* was sent to Westerbork shortly after the rest of the family was sent to Auschwitz. From Westerbork, Jaap was sent to Bergen-Belsen concentration camp in February 1944. As the Allies closed in on the Third Reich in April 1945, Bergen-Belsen was partially evacuated by the Nazis, and Jaap was put on a train going east under conditions of extreme deprivation and hardship. The train was liberated by the Soviet Army, but Jaap's physical condition was such that he died shortly afterward. He was the last of Etty's immediate family to die.[343]

Viktor Frankl had been practicing neurology and psychiatry in Vienna when he was arrested by the Nazis, and he returned to that practice after the war. He founded the logotherapy method in psychiatry, which is based on the principle that a person must have meaning in life in order to have true fulfillment and happiness. His first wife perished in the Holocaust; in 1947 he married a Catholic woman, and they attended both synagogue services and Mass on a regular basis. He died in Vienna in 1997 at the age of ninety-two. By then he had published some thirty-nine books.

Linda Breder returned to her native Stropkov in Czechoslovakia only to find that her family home had been confiscated by the Soviets and given to another family. "Go back to where you came from," the owner said as he slammed the door in her face.[344] She met her husband in a bread line in Czechoslovakia. The couple eventually immigrated to San Francisco, California, where she became a Holocaust speaker, addressing scores of audiences over the years. She returned to Auschwitz-Birkenau four times with groups of young people, and she was able to point out the exact bunk where she and eight other girls had slept. Breder believed there was no God in Auschwitz. "There were such horrible conditions that God decided not to go there," she said. "We didn't pray because we knew it wouldn't help. Many of us who survived are atheists. They simply don't trust in God."[345] Breder died in San Francisco in 2010 at the age of eighty-six.

Alice Lok Cahana survived the death march when the Nazis moved thousands of prisoners to Bergen-Belsen because the Soviet forces were closing in on Auschwitz-Birkenau in 1945. After Bergen-Belsen was liberated in 1945, she moved to a Swedish rehabilitation center and then to Israel where she met her husband, a rabbi. Eventually they moved to Houston, Texas, where Cahana became an internationally celebrated artist of the Holocaust. In 2006, she presented one of her paintings to Pope Benedict XVI at the Vatican. Titled *No Names*, it is a dark, abstract work depicting her first hours in Auschwitz. The canvas is covered with numbers, emphasizing the prisoners' loss of identity. That painting is the only piece of Holocaust art in the Vatican Museum. Cahana died in 2017 at the age of eighty-eight.

Thomas Blatt was among the three hundred prisoners who escaped from Sobibor in October 1943. (Many were recaptured or killed by the German search squads.) After the war, he lived first in his native Poland and later in Israel. In 1958 he immigrated to the United States and settled in Santa Barbara, California. Throughout his life, he did extensive research on Holocaust survivors and wrote two books on the subject. He was a consultant for the 1987 television film *Escape from Sobibor*. He died in 2018 at the age of eighty-eight.

Otto Pressburger was among the first Jews to arrive in Auschwitz in April 1942. His brother Aladar and family arrived three months later, but did not recognize Otto because of his deteriorated physical condition. Otto finally sang a childhood song to convince his brother of his identity. In January 1945, when Auschwitz was being evacuated by the Nazis, Pressburger was put on a train headed for Austria. As they were passing through Czech territory, he jumped from the train and pretended to be dead. After the war, he went to Israel where he fought in the War of Independence. At the time of this writing, he is living in Israel.

Rudolf Höss disguised himself and worked as a gardener under an assumed name for several months after the war. When he was finally tracked down by British authorities, he tried to bite into a cyanide pill but was stopped by his captors. Eventually he was tried for murder by the Supreme National Tribunal of Poland and hanged on 16 April 1947. He was forty-five years old. The gallows was erected next to the first crematorium in the original Auschwitz extermination camp, the crematorium that was eventually replaced by the Little Red House in Birkenau. While in prison, Höss wrote a memoir that is conspicuously self-serving, but is nonetheless considered an important document on the Holocaust. Before his execution, he returned to the Catholic Church and received the last sacraments.

Acknowledgments

I am indebted to my bishop, the Most Rev. Jaime Soto, for his friendly support and encouragement throughout the writing process. I am also indebted to John Martino, acquisitions editor at Catholic University of America Press, who recommended my manuscript to New City Press. I also owe a debt of gratitude to the many friends who were willing to read the manuscript and make so many valuable suggestions: Bishop William Weigand; Bishop Tom Curry; Msgr. Albert O'Connor; Sr. Maureen McInerney, O.P.; Sr. Maura Power, S.M.; Sr. Kathleen Horgan, S.M.; Deacon Eric Hintz; Ronda Hintz; and Loretta Olson. It was Loretta who carefully took note of the dozens of typos that needed fixing before the manuscript was finalized. Claire Perez came to my rescue when I needed to do something on the computer that was above my pay grade: turning all the footnotes into endnotes, for example.

I am also grateful to my first cousin, Sr. Geraldine Collins, S.M., whose gift of a book for my 50th anniversary of ordination sparked my interest in Etty Hillesum. That book put me on a fascinating journey: first getting to know Etty through her diary, and then getting better acquainted with many of the authors who formed her: Rainer Maria Rilke, Fyodor Dostoevsky, Carl Jung, St. Augustine, and Meister Eckhart. Finally, I am also grateful to the hero of this book, Etty Hillesum herself, who has become such a significant presence in my life these past three years. Surprising as it may seem, I feel as close to her as I do to my favorite saints (including St. Edith Stein), even though Etty is not an officially canonized saint.

Selected Bibliography

Augustine of Hippo. *Confessions.* New York: Penguin Books, 1961.

Barry, William, S.J. *God's Passionate Desire.* Chicago: Loyola Press, 2008.

Dostoevsky, Fyodor. *The Brothers Karamazov.* New York: Signet Classics, 2007. (Note: first published in Russian in 1879)

Dwyer, Jean Marie, O.P. *The Unfolding Journey. The God Within: Etty Hillesum & Meister Eckhart.* Toronto: Novalis, 2014.

Frankl, Victor. *Man's Search For Meaning.* Boston: Beacon Press, 2006. (Note: first published in German in 1946)

Hamans, Father Paul. *Edith Stein and Companions: On the Way to Auschwitz.* San Francisco: Ignatius Press, 2010.

Herbstrith, Waltraud, O.C.D. *Edith Stein: A Biography.* San Francisco: Ignatius Press, 1992.

Hillesum, Etty. *An Interrupted Life: The Diaries 1941-1943 and Letters from Westerbork.* New York: Henry Holt and Company, 1996.

Hillesum, Etty. *Etty: The Letters and Diaries of Etty Hillesum 1941-1943. Complete and unabridged.* Grand Rapids: William B. Eerdmans Publishing Company, 2002.

Laqueur, Walter, ed. *The Holocaust Encyclopedia.* New Haven: Yale University Press, 2001.

Maas, Frans. *Spirituality as Insight: Mystical Texts and Theological Reflection.* Leuven; Paris; Dudley, MA: Peeters, 2004.

Mosley, Joanne. *Edith Stein: Modern Saint and Martyr*. New Jersey: HiddenSpring, 2004.

Rees, Laurence. *Auschwitz: The Nazis & the 'Final Solution'*. BBC Books, 2005.

Smelik, Klaas A. D., Meins G. S. Coetsier, and Jurjen Wiersma, eds. *The Ethics and Religious Philosophy of Etty Hillesum: Proceedings of the Etty Hillesum Conference at Ghent University, January 2014*. Leiden: Brill, 2017.

Smelik, Klaas A. D., ed. *The Lasting Significance of Etty Hillesum's Writings: Proceedings of the Etty Hillesum Conference at Middelburg, September 2018*. Amsterdam: Amsterdam University Press, 2019.

Smelik, Klaas A. D., Ria van den Brandt, and Meins G. S. Coetsier, eds. *Spirituality in the Writings of Etty Hillesum: Proceedings of the Etty Hillesum Conference at Ghent University, November 2008*. Leiden: Brill, 2010.

Woodhouse, Patrick. *Etty Hillesum: A Life Transformed*. New York: Bloomsbury, 2009.

Notes

Introduction

1. William A. Barry, S.J., *God's Passionate Desire* (Chicago: Loyola Press, 2008), 76–85.

2. Etty Hillesum, *Etty: The Letters and Diaries of Etty Hillesum 1941-1943, Complete and Unabridged*, ed. Klaas A. D. Smelik, trans. Arnold J. Pomerans (Grand Rapids: Wm. B. Eerdmans, 2002), 434.

3. Hillesum, *Letters and Diaries*, 616.

4. Elie Wiesel, *Night* (New York: Hill and Wang, 2006), 67, 68.

5. Quoted in Roy H. Schoeman, *Salvation Is from the Jews* (San Francisco: Ignatius Press, 2003), 154.

6. Quoted in Schoeman, *Salvation*, 143.

7. Hillesum, *Letters and Diaries*, 487.

8. Hillesum, *Letters and Diaries*, 506.

9. Jan G. Gaarlandt, "Context, Dilemmas, and Misunderstanding During the Composition and Publication of *An Interrupted Life: Etty Hillesum's Diary, 1941-1943*," in *Spirituality in the Writings of Etty Hillesum: Proceedings of the Etty Hillesum Conference at Ghent University November 2008*, eds. Klaas A. D. Smelik, Ria van den Brandt, and Meins G. S. Coetsier (Leiden: Brill, 2010), 365.

10. Etty Hillesum, *An Interrupted Life: The Diaries 1941-1943 and Letters from Westerbork*, ed. Jan G. Gaarlandt (New York: Henry Holt and Company, 1996), xxiii.

11. Benedict XVI, General Audience, February 13, 2013.

12. Lucetta Scaraffia, *Que viste no meu rosto? O encontro de Edith Stein e Etty Hillesum no campo holandés de Westerbork*, in *L'Osservatore Romano*, August 8, 2012.

13. Hillesum, *Letters and Diaries*, 524.

14. Harriet Sherwood, "Nearly two-thirds of US young adults unaware 6m Jews killed in the Holocaust," *The Guardian*, September 16, 2020, www.theguardian.com/world/2020/sep/16/holocaust-us-adults-study.

15. Melissa Eddy, "Vandals Tag 9 Barracks at Auschwitz with Anti-Semitic slurs," *New York Times*, October 6, 2021.

16. Cf. Ria van den Brandt, "Etty Hillesum and her 'Catholic Worshippers': A Plea for a More Critical Approach to Etty Hillesum's Writings," in Smelik et al., *Spirituality in the Writings of Etty Hillesum*, 215–231.

17. See Rachel Feldhay Brenner, "Etty Hillesum: A Portrait of a Holocaust Artist," in Smelik et al., *Spirituality in the Writings of Etty Hillesum*, 239.

18. Hillesum, *Letters and Diaries*, 465.

19. Jean Marie Dwyer, O.P., *The Unfolding Journey: The God Within: Etty Hillesum & Meister Eckhart* (Toronto: Novalis, 2014), 18.

20. *The New Dictionary of Theology*, eds. Joseph A. Komonchak, Mary Collins, Dermot A. Lane (Wilmington: Michael Glazier, 1987), 694.

21. *Sacramentum Mundi, An Encyclopedia of Theology*, Volume IV, ed. Karl Rahner, S.J. (New York: Herder and Herder, 1969), 138.

22. Rahner, *Sacramentum Mundi*, IV, 138.

A Note on the Word "Holocaust"

23. Walter Laqueur and Judith Tydor Baumel, eds., *The Holocaust Encyclopedia*, (New Haven, CT: Yale University Press, 2001), xiii.

Chapter 1

24. Hillesum, *Interrupted Life*, xvi.

25. Klaas A. D. Smelik, "A Short Biography of Etty Hillesum (1914-1943)," in Smelik et al., *Spirituality in the Writings of Etty Hillesum*, 22.

26. Hillesum, *Interrupted Life*, xvi.

27. Hillesum, *Interrupted Life*, xvii.

28. Hillesum, *Interrupted Life*, viii.

29. Hillesum, *Interrupted Life*, xvi.

30. Patrick Woodhouse, "The Influence of the Work of Rainer Maria Rilke on the Mind and Heart of Etty Hillesum," in *The Ethics and Religious Philosophy of Etty Hillesum: Proceedings of the Etty Hillesum Conference at Ghent University, January 2014*, eds. Klaas A. D. Smelik, Meins G. S. Coetsier, and Jurjen Wiersma (Leiden: Brill, 2017), 285, 286.

31. Hillesum, *Letters and Diaries*, 674.

32. Hillesum, *Letters and Diaries*, 674.

33. Hillesum, *Letters and Diaries*, 735.

34. Hillesum, *Letters and Diaries*, 6.

35. Hillesum, *Letters and Diaries*, 6, 7.

36. Hillesum, *Letters and Diaries*, 4.

37. Maria Clara Lucchetti Bingemer, "The Journey of Etty Hillesum from Eros to Agape," in Smelik et al., *Ethics and Religious Philosophy*, 72.

38. See Jan G. Gaarlandt, "Context, Dilemmas, and Misunderstandings," in Smelik et al., *Spirituality in the Writings of Etty Hillesum*, 375.

39. Gaarlandt, "Context, Dilemmas, and Misunderstandings," in Smelik et al., *Spirituality in the Writings of Etty Hillesum*, 374.
40. Gaarlandt, "Context, Dilemmas, and Misunderstandings," in Smelik et al., *Spirituality in the Writings of Etty Hillesum*, 375.
41. See Hillesum, *Letters and Diaries*, 767.
42. Hillesum, *Letters and Diaries*, 7.
43. Hillesum, *Letters and Diaries*, 320, 448.
44. Hillesum, *Letters and Diaries*, 585.
45. Hillesum, *Letters and Diaries*, 71.
46. Hillesum, *Letters and Diaries*, 544.
47. Hillesum, *Letters and Diaries*, 154.
48. Cf. Woodhouse, "Rainer Maria Rilke," in Smelik et al., *Ethics and Religious Philosophy*.
49. Hillesum, *Letters and Diaries*, 543, 546; Rainer Maria Rilke, *The Book of Hours*, ed. Ben Hutchinson, trans. Susan Ranson (Rochester: Camden House, 2008), 231.
50. See Wil van den Bercken, "Etty Hillesum's Russian Vocation and Spiritual Relationship to Dostoevsky," in Smelik et al., *Spirituality in the Writings of Etty Hillesum*, 157.
51. Van den Bercken, "Russian Vocation," in Smelik et al., *Spirituality in the Writings of Etty Hillesum*, 147.
52. Hillesum, *Letters and Diaries*, 214.
53. Hillesum, *Letters and Diaries*, 494.
54. Hillesum, *Letters and Diaries*, 4.
55. Hillesum, *Letters and Diaries*, 60.
56. Hillesum, *Letters and Diaries*, 126.
57. Augustine of Hippo, *Confessions*, Book 1, Chapter 1.
58. Hillesum, *Letters and Diaries*, 385, 386.
59. Augustine, *Confessions*, viii, 5.
60. Hillesum, *Letters and Diaries*, 466.
61. Hillesum, *Letters and Diaries*, 175.
62. Hillesum, *Letters and Diaries*, 529.
63. Spier also introduced Etty to St. Francis of Assisi and Thomas à Kempis.
64. Hillesum, *Letters and Diaries*, 473.
65. Hillesum, *Letters and Diaries*, 473.
66. Hillesum, *Letters and Diaries*, 657.
67. Hillesum, *Letters and Diaries*, 526.
68. Hillesum, *Letters and Diaries*, 458.
69. Hillesum, *Letters and Diaries*, 455, 737.
70. Hillesum, *Letters and Diaries*, 761.

71. Patrick Woodhouse, *Etty Hillesum, A Life Transformed* (New York: Bloomsbury, 2009), 88.

72. Hillesum, *Letters and Diaries*, 399.

73. Brenner, "Portrait of a Holocaust Artist," in Smelik et al., *Spirituality in the Writings of Etty Hillesum*, 244.

74. Hillesum, *Letters and Diaries*, 485, 486, 487.

75. Hillesum, *Letters and Diaries*, 489.

76. Hillesum, *Letters and Diaries*, 580.

77. Hillesum, *Letters and Diaries*, 620.

78. Hillesum, *Letters and Diaries*, 583.

79. Hillesum, *Letters and Diaries*, 588.

80. Hillesum, *Letters and Diaries*, 584.

81. Hillesum, *Letters and Diaries*, 583.

82. Hillesum, *Letters and Diaries*, 590.

83. Hillesum, *Letters and Diaries*, 768. Friedrich Weinreb later became famous because of the "Weinreb Lists" scandal. He drew up lists guaranteeing Jews protection from extermination if they paid him a fee. It was a scam.

84. Meins G. S. Coetsier, "'You-Consciousness'—Towards Political Theory: Etty Hillesum's Experience and Symbolization of the Divine Presence," in Smelik et al., *Spirituality in the Writings of Etty Hillesum*, 105, 106. Coetsier is a permanent deacon in the Diocese of Fulda in Germany.

Chapter 2

85. See Augustine, *Confessions*, 11.

86. Hillesum, *Letters and Diaries*, 4.

87. Hillesum, *Letters and Diaries*, 92.

88. Hillesum, *Letters and Diaries*, 458.

89. Hillesum, *Letters and Diaries*, 93.

90. Hillesum, *Letters and Diaries*, 682.

91. Hillesum, *Letters and Diaries*, 83.

92. Hillesum, *Letters and Diaries*, 79, 80.

93. Hillesum, *Letters and Diaries*, x, xi.

94. Hillesum, *Letters and Diaries*, 160.

95. Woodhouse, *Life Transformed*, 7.

96. Hillesum, *Interrupted Life*, xvi.

97. Woodhouse, *Life Transformed*, 7.

98. Hillesum, *Letters and Diaries*, 86.

99. Woodhouse, *Life Transformed*, 11.

100. Hillesum, *Letters and Diaries*, 146.

101. Hillesum, *Letters and Diaries*, 146.

102. Hillesum, *Letters and Diaries*, 83.

103. Hillesum, *Letters and Diaries*, 198, 199.

104. Hillesum, *Letters and Diaries*, 341.

105. Patrick Woodhouse, "The Roots of the Chaos and the Process of Change in Etty Hillesum," in Smelik et al., *Spirituality in the Writings of Etty Hillesum*, 36.

106. Hillesum, *Letters and Diaries*, 7.

107. Hillesum, *Letters and Diaries*, 42, 43.

108. Hillesum, *Letters and Diaries*, 141.

109. Hillesum, *Letters and Diaries*, xi.

110. Hillesum, *Letters and Diaries*, 249.

111. Hillesum, *Letters and Diaries*, 88.

112. Hillesum, *Letters and Diaries*, 168.

113. Hillesum, *Letters and Diaries*, 3.

114. Hillesum, *Letters and Diaries*, 55.

115. Hillesum, *Letters and Diaries*, 8

116. Hillesum, *Letters and Diaries*, 8.

117. Hillesum, *Letters and Diaries*, 386.

118. Hillesum, *Letters and Diaries*, 3.

119. Hillesum, *Letters and Diaries*, 92.

120. Hillesum, *Letters and Diaries*, 278.

121. Hillesum, *Letters and Diaries*, 355.

122. Woodhouse, *Life Transformed*, 22.

123. Hillesum, *Letters and Diaries*, 323.

124. Hillesum, *Letters and Diaries*, 84.

125. Hillesum, *Letters and Diaries*, 162.

126. Hillesum, *Letters and Diaries*, 558. By "antenna" she meant a hearing aid.

127. Quoted in Alexandra Pleshoyano, "Etty Hillesum and Julius Spier: A 'Spierituality' on the Fringe of Religious Borders," in Smelik et al., *Spirituality in the Writings of Etty Hillesum*, 62.

128. Hillesum, *Letters and Diaries*, 411.

129. Hillesum, *Letters and Diaries*, 252, 253.

Chapter 3

130. Benedict XVI, General Audience, 13 February 2013.

131. Hillesum, *Letters and Diaries*, 42.

132. Hillesum, *Letters and Diaries*, 25, 26.

133. Hillesum, *Letters and Diaries*, 126.

134. Hillesum, *Letters and Diaries*, 122.

135. Hillesum, *Letters and Diaries*, 516.

136. Hillesum, *Letters and Diaries*, 56, 57.

137. Hillesum, *Letters and Diaries*, 42.

138. Hillesum, *Letters and Diaries*, 439–440, 494, 519.

139. Hillesum, *Letters and Diaries*, 103.

140. Hillesum, *Letters and Diaries*, 547.

141. Hillesum, *Letters and Diaries*, 181.

142. Hillesum, *Letters and Diaries*, 320.

143. Hillesum, *Letters and Diaries*, 497.

144. Hillesum, *Letters and Diaries*, 148.

145. Marja Clement, "The Girl Who Could Not Kneel," in *The Lasting Significance of Etty Hillesum's Writings: Proceedings of the Etty Hillesum Conference at Middelburg, September 2018*, ed. Klaas A. D. Smelik (Amsterdam: Amsterdam University Press, 2019), 147–155.

146. Hillesum, *Letters and Diaries*, 256, 290, 301, 496, 497. De Jonge rented a room in the same building as Spier.

147. Hillesum, *Letters and Diaries*, 198.

148. Hillesum, *Letters and Diaries*, 197, 198.

149. Hillesum, *Letters and Diaries*, 198. See also Clement, "Kneel," in Smelik, *Lasting Significance*, 151.

150. Hillesum, *Letters and Diaries*, 106.

151. Hillesum, *Letters and Diaries*, 351. Etty quotes two paragraphs from Rilke.

152. Hillesum, *Letters and Diaries*, 204.

153. Hillesum, *Letters and Diaries*, 154.

154. Hillesum, *Letters and Diaries*, 364.

155. Fyodor Dostoevsky, *The Brothers Karamazov* (New York: Signet Classics, 2007), Book v, Chapter 4.

156. Dostoevsky, *Karamazov*, v, 4.

157. Dostoevsky, *Karamazov*, v, 4.

158. Dostoevsky, *Karamazov*, v, 4.

159. Dostoevsky, *Karamazov*, v, 5.

160. Dostoevsky, *Karamazov*, v, 5.

161. See van den Bercken, "Russian Vocation," in Smelik et al., *Spirituality in the Writings of Etty Hillesum*, 163.

162. Van den Bercken, "Russian Vocation," in Smelik et al., *Spirituality in the Writings of Etty Hillesum*, 162. We are using the van den Bercken translation. Note that for Etty, God seems to have an abstract image in this diary entry, a Creator who suffers for his creation rather than Christ suffering on the Cross.

163. Hillesum, *Letters and Diaries*, 455, 456.

164. Dostoevsky, *Karamazov*, Book vi, 1. Father Zosima's spirituality is often compared to that of St. Francis of Assisi, who was also a favorite of Etty Hillesum.

165. Dostoevsky, *Karamazov*, vi, 2.

166. Dostoevsky, *Karamazov*, vi, 1.

167. Dostoevsky, *Karamazov*, vi, 1.

168. See van den Bercken, "Russian Vocation," in Smelik et al., *Spirituality in the Writings of Etty Hillesum*, 166.

169. Hillesum, *Letters and Diaries*, 515.

170. Hillesum, *Letters and Diaries*, 68.

171. Hillesum, *Letters and Diaries*, 307.

172. Van den Bercken, "Russian Vocation," in Smelik et al., *Spirituality in the Writings of Etty Hillesum*, 162.

173. Hillesum, *Letters and Diaries*, 515.

174. Van den Bercken, "Russian Vocation," in Smelik et al., *Spirituality in the Writings of Etty Hillesum*, 170.

Chapter 4

175. Hillesum, *Letters and Diaries*, 640.

176. Hillesum, *Letters and Diaries*, 529.

177. Hillesum, *Letters and Diaries*, 616.

178. See Galatians 5:22.

179. Dwyer, *Unfolding Journey*, 34.

180. Francesca Brezzi, "Etty Hillesum, An 'Atypical' Mystic," in Smelik et al., *Spirituality in the Writings of Etty Hillesum*, 174. She is quoting another theologian, Antonietta Potente.

181. Hillesum, *Letters and Diaries*, 461, 463.

182. Etty quotes a poem from Rilke (*Letters and Diaries*, 276) that uses the word *Weltinnenraum*. However, for Etty, *Weltinnenraum* has a special connection to suffering. See Maria Gabriella Nocita, "Feeling Life: Etty Hillesum Becomes Word," in Smelik et al., *Spirituality in the Writings of Etty Hillesum*, 282.

183. Hillesum, *Letters and Diaries*, 433.

184. Hillesum, *Letters and Diaries*, 4.

185. Hillesum, *Letters and Diaries*, 586.

186. Hillesum, *Letters and Diaries*, 474.

187. Hillesum, *Letters and Diaries*, 466.

188. Hillesum, *Letters and Diaries*, 526, 527.

189. Hillesum, *Letters and Diaries*, 349, 452, 459.

190. Hillesum, *Letters and Diaries*, 386.

191. Hillesum, *Letters and Diaries*, 453.

192. See van den Bercken, "Russian Vocation," in Smelik et al., *Spirituality in the Writings of Etty Hillesum*, 152.

193. Hillesum, *Letters and Diaries*, 183.

194. Hillesum, *Letters and Diaries*, 183.

195. Wiesel, *Night*, xxi.

196. Hillesum, *Letters and Diaries*, 109.

197. Hillesum, *Letters and Diaries*, 111.

198. Hillesum, *Letters and Diaries*, 112.

199. Hillesum, *Letters and Diaries*, 113.

200. Hillesum, *Letters and Diaries*, 113.

201. Hillesum, *Letters and Diaries*, 466.

202. Hillesum, *Letters and Diaries*, 113.

203. Hillesum, *Letters and Diaries*, 259.

204. Hillesum, *Letters and Diaries*, 19.

205. Hillesum, *Letters and Diaries*, 18.

206. Hillesum, *Letters and Diaries*, 18.

207. Hillesum, *Letters and Diaries*, 259.

208. Hillesum, *Letters and Diaries*, 258.

209. Hillesum, *Letters and Diaries*, 259.

210. Hillesum, *Letters and Diaries*, 181.

211. Hillesum, *Letters and Diaries*, 19.

212. Hillesum, *Letters and Diaries*, 529.

213. Hillesum, *Letters and Diaries*, 517.

214. Paul Lebeau, "The Reception of Etty Hillesum's Writings in French Language," in Smelik et al., *Spirituality in the Writings of Etty Hillesum*, 212.

215. Hillesum, *Letters and Diaries*, 744.

216. Hillesum, *Letters and Diaries*, 256.

217. Hillesum, *Letters and Diaries*, 590, 591.

218. Hillesum, *Letters and Diaries*, 532.

219. Ria van den Brandt, "Now is the Time to Put into Practice: Love Your Enemies," in Smelik, *Lasting Significance*, 87.

220. Van den Brandt, "Love Your Enemies," in Smelik, *Lasting Significance*, 88.

221. Hillesum, *Letters and Diaries*, 541.

222. Hillesum, *Letters and Diaries*, 542, 543.

223. Hillesum, *Letters and Diaries*, 461.

224. Hillesum, *Letters and Diaries*, 463.

225. See Rilke, *Book of Hours*, 163.

226. Hillesum, *Letters and Diaries*, 464.

227. Pope Benedict XVI, *Deus Caritas Est*, December 25, 2005, https://www.vatican.va/content/benedict-xvi/en/encyclicals/documents/hf_ben-xvi_enc_20051225_deus-caritas-est.html, paragraph 1.

228. Benedict XVI, *Deus Caritas Est*, 1.

229. Benedict XVI, *Deus Caritas Est*, 4.

230. Benedict XVI, *Deus Caritas Est*, 4.

231. Benedict XVI, *Deus Caritas Est*, 5.

232. Benedict XVI, *Deus Caritas Est*, 6.

233. Bingemer, "Eros to Agape," in Smelik et al., *Ethics and Religious Philosophy*, 68–89.

234. Bingemer, "Eros to Agape," in Smelik et al., *Ethics and Religious Philosophy*, 73. Bingemer also quotes Gregory of Nyssa, a Church Father of the fourth century, who preferred the word *eros* to *agape* when describing mystical experiences. He defined *eros* as a more intense *agape*.

235. Bingemer, "Eros to Agape," in Smelik et al., *Ethics and Religious Philosophy*, 74.

236. Hillesum, *Letters and Diaries*, 359, 360.

237. Bingemer, "Eros to Agape," in Smelik et al., *Ethics and Religious Philosophy*, 76.

238. Bingemer, "Eros to Agape," in Smelik et al., *Ethics and Religious Philosophy*, 89.

239. Hillesum, *Letters and Diaries*, 550.

240. Hillesum, *Letters and Diaries*, 549.

241. Cf. van den Brandt, "Catholic Worshippers," in Smelik et al., *Spirituality in the Writings of Etty Hillesum*, 215–231.

242. Bingemer, "Eros to Agape," in Smelik et al., *Ethics and Religious Philosophy*, 79.

243. Hillesum, *Letters and Diaries*, 666.

244. Hillesum, *Letters and Diaries*, 782.

245. Hillesum, *Letters and Diaries*, 773.

246. Hillesum, *Letters and Diaries*, 667.

247. Hillesum, *Letters and Diaries*, 667.

248. Hillesum, *Letters and Diaries*, 668.

249. Hillesum, *Letters and Diaries*, 668.

250. Etty seems to be paraphrasing the first two verses of Psalm 18.

251. Hillesum, *Letters and Diaries*, 658, 659.

Chapter 5

252. Lebeau, "Reception in French Language," in Smelik et al., *Spirituality in the Writings of Etty Hillesum*, 207.

253. Waltraud Herbstrith, *Edith Stein: A Biography* (San Francisco: Ignatius Press, 1992), 33.

254. Herbstrith, *Stein*, 39.

255. The young Karol Wojtyla wrote his dissertation on Max Scheler and, as Pope John Paul II, he canonized Edith Stein in 1998.

256. Herbstrith, *Stein*, 47.

257. Herbstrith, *Stein*, 61.

258. Quoted in Herbstrith, *Stein*, 48.

259. Herbstrith, *Stein*, 50.

260. Quoted in Herbstrith, *Stein*, 49, 50.

261. Herbstrith, *Stein*, 65.

262. Quoted in Herbstrith, *Stein*, 67.

263. Herbstrith, *Stein*, 81.

264. Quoted in Edith Stein, *The Science of the Cross* (Washington: ICS Publications, 2002), xvii, xviii.

265. Joanne Mosley, *Edith Stein: Modern Saint and Martyr* (New Jersey: HiddenSpring, 2006), 37

266. Quoted in Herbstrith, *Stein*, 167.

267. Quoted in Mosley, *Modern Saint*, 44.

268. Quoted in Herbstrith, *Stein*, 165.

269. The Schutzstaffel, or SS, was the elite corps of highly trained officers in charge of national security and the concentration camps.

270. Rosa, a Third Order Carmelite, was the convent cook at this time, and as such was provided with a room in the abbey compound.

271. Father Paul Hamans, *Edith Stein and Companions: On the Way to Auschwitz* (San Francisco: Ignatius Press, 2010), 81.

272. Quoted in Hamans, *On the Way*, 80.

273. Quoted in Hamans, *On the Way*, 82.

274. Herbstrith, *Stein*, 180.

275. Mosley, *Modern Saint*, 51.

276. Herbstrith, *Stein*, 182.

277. Quoted in Herbstrith, *Stein*, 183.

278. Hillesum, *Letters and Diaries*, 585.

279. His name was Fr. George Loeb. He was one of five members of the Loeb family, all of whom were Trappists and all of whom perished in Auschwitz: two priests, two nuns, and one lay brother. The two nuns were gassed as soon as they arrived in Auschwitz; the three men were sent to slave labor units and, presumably, died the slow death of starvation and abuse. See Hamans, *Stein*, 154–180.

280. Hillesum, *Letters and Diaries*, 585, 586

281. Hillesum, *Letters and Diaries*, 586.

282. Hamans, *On the Way*, 86.

283. Quoted in Herbstrith, *Stein*, 192. This recollection, based on one man's memory, cannot be confirmed by other sources.

284. A spur track had been built to connect the newly opened Birkenau facility with the main railway line.

285. Quoted in Laurence Rees, *Auschwitz: The Nazis & the 'Final Solution'* (Great Britain: BBC Books, 2005), 259, 260. This is the companion book to the BBC documentary series of the same name.

286. Quoted in Rees, *Auschwitz*, 144.

287. Laqueur and Baumel, *Holocaust Encyclopedia*, 718.

288. Christiana Dobner, "75eme anniversaire de la mort d'Edith Stein dans L'Osservatore Romano," Zenit News Agency, August 8, 2017.

289. *Shema Yisrael* are the first two words of a section in the Torah (Deuteronomy 6:4–9). The words also refer to the central prayer that is used during Jewish morning and evening prayer services.

290. Hillesum, *Letters and Diaries*, 26.

291. Hillesum, *Letters and Diaries*, 126.

292. Quoted in Herbstrith, *Stein*, 60.

293. Hillesum, *Letters and Diaries*, 464.

294. Quoted in Schoeman, *Salvation*, 163.

295. Hillesum, *Letters and Diaries*, 435.

296. Mosley, *Modern Saint*, 47.

297. Hillesum, *Letters and Diaries*, 91.

298. Quoted in Herbstrith, *Stein*, 157.

299. Hillesum, *Letters and Diaries*, 607.

300. Hillesum, *Letters and Diaries*, 640.

301. Herbstrith, *Stein*, 183.

302. Quoted in Herbstrith, *Stein*, 185.

303. Hillesum, *Letters and Diaries*, 529.

304. Quoted in Herbstrith, *Stein*, 194.

305. Hillesum, *Letters and Diaries*, 761.

306. Quoted in Herbstrith, *Stein*, 169.

307. Quoted in Herbstrith, *Stein*, 180.

Chapter 6

308. Wiesel, *Night*, 28.

309. Rudolf Höss, *Death Dealer: The Memoirs of the SS Kommandant at Auschwitz* (Buffalo: Da Capo Press, 1996), 159, 160.

310. Rees, *Auschwitz*, 100.

311. Laqueur and Baumel, *Holocaust Encyclopedia*, 38.

312. Rees, *Auschwitz*, 252.

313. Quoted in Rees, *Auschwitz*, 32.

314. Quoted in Rees, *Auschwitz*, 139, 140.

315. Laqueur and Baumel, *Holocaust Encyclopedia*, 41.

316. Viktor Frankl, *Man's Search For Meaning* (Boston: Beacon Press, 2006), 29.

317. Höss, *Death Dealer*, 133.

318. Robert Rozett and Shmuel Spector, eds., *Encyclopedia of the Holocaust* (Jerusalem: Yad Vashem, 2000), 67.

319. Frankl, *Meaning*, 30.

320. Quoted in Rees, *Auschwitz*, 101.

321. Rozett and Spector, *Encyclopedia*, 67.

322. Frankl, *Meaning*, 28, 29.

323. Quoted in Rees, *Auschwitz*, 320.

324. Rozett and Spector, *Encyclopedia*, 67.

325. Quoted in Rees, *Auschwitz*, 224.

326. Höss, *Death Dealer*, 22.

327. Quoted in Rees, *Auschwitz*, 225.

328. Hillesum, *Letters and Diaries*, 476.

329. Rees, *Auschwitz*, 250.

330. Frankl, *Meaning*, 50.

331. Frankl, *Meaning*, 66.

332. Frankl, *Meaning*, 37.

333. Frankl, *Meaning*, 37.

334. Frankl, *Meaning*, 37.

335. Frankl, *Meaning*, 39, 40.

336. Frankl, *Meaning*, 74.

337. Frankl, *Meaning*, 67.

338. Hillesum, *Letters and Diaries*, 464.

339. Hillesum, *Letters and Diaries*, 480.

340. Hillesum, *Letters and Diaries*, 487.

341. Annotation in Hillesum, *Letters and Diaries*, 783.

342. Hillesum, *Letters and Diaries*, 474.

Epilogue

343. Smelik, "Short Biography," in Smelik et al., *Spirituality in the Writings of Etty Hillesum*, 27.

344. Quoted in Rees, *Auschwitz*, 348.

345. Quoted in Rees, *Auschwitz*, 373, 374.

New City Press

New City Press is one of more than 20 publishing houses sponsored by the Focolare, a movement founded by Chiara Lubich to help bring about the realization of Jesus' prayer: "That all may be one" (John 17:21). In view of that goal, New City Press publishes books and resources that enrich the lives of people and help all to strive toward the unity of the entire human family. We are a member of the Association of Catholic Publishers.

www.newcitypress.com
202 Comforter Blvd.
Hyde Park, New York

Periodicals
Living City Magazine
www.livingcitymagazine.com

Scan to join our mailing list
for discounts and promotions
or go to www.newcitypress.com
and click on "join our email list."